SCHOLASTIC

BOOK
OF
WORLD
RECORDS
2009

by Jenifer Corr Morse
A GEORGIAN BAY BOOK

To Isabelle Nicole—May you always find wonder in the world.
—JCM

CREATED AND PRODUCED BY GEORGIAN BAY ASSOCIATES, LLC

GEORGIAN BAY STAFF
Bruce S. Glassman, Executive Editor
Jenifer Corr Morse, Photo Editor

SCHOLASTIC STAFF
Brenda Murray, Editor
Trevor Ingerson, Intern
Becky Terhune, Art Director
Kay Petronio, Designer
Susan Schultz, Cover designer

In most cases, the graphs in this book represent the top five record holders in each category. However, in some graphs, we have chosen to list well-known or common people, places, animals, or things that will help you better understand how extraordinary the record holder is. These may not be the top five in the category. Additionally, some graphs have fewer than five entries because so few people or objects reflect the necessary criteria.

ISBN-13: 978-0-545-08211-2
ISBN-10: 0-545-08211-0

10 9 8 7 6 5 4 3 2 1   08 09 10 11 12
Printed in the U.S.A.   23
First printing, September 2008

CONTENTS

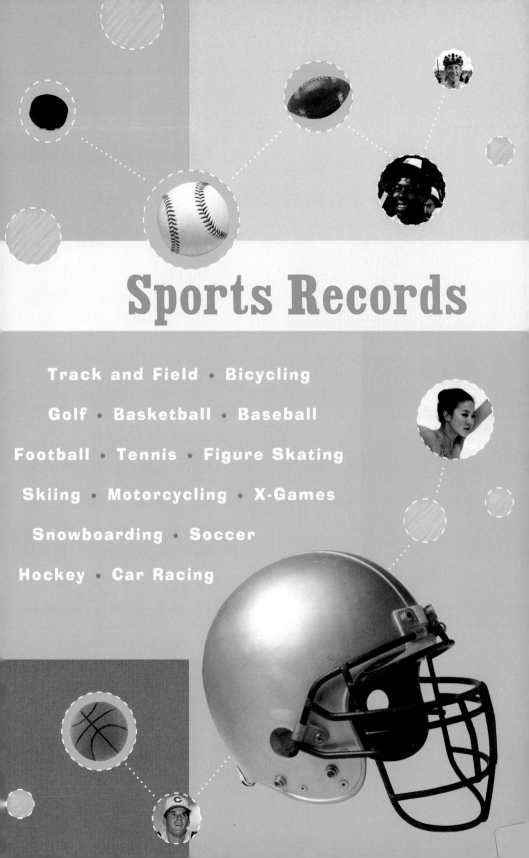

Sports Records

Track and Field • Bicycling

Golf • Basketball • Baseball

Football • Tennis • Figure Skating

Skiing • Motorcycling • X-Games

Snowboarding • Soccer

Hockey • Car Racing

6

Runner with the
World's

FASTEST MILE

Hicham El Guerrouj

Moroccan runner HICHAM EL GUERROUJ
is super speedy—he ran a mile in just over 3
minutes and 43 seconds in July 1999 while
racing in Rome. He also holds the record for
the fastest mile in North America with a time
just short of 3 minutes and 50 seconds. El
Guerrouj is also an Olympian with gold medals
in the 1500-meter and 5000-meter races. With
this accomplishment at the 2004 Athens Games,
he became the first runner to win both races at
the same Olympics in more than 75 years. El
Guerrouj returned to the Olympics in 2006 as a
torchbearer in Torino, Italy.

RUNNERS WITH THE WORLD'S FASTEST MILE

Time, in minutes and seconds

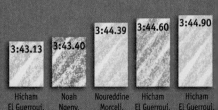

3:43.13	3:43.40	3:44.39	3:44.60	3:44.90
Hicham El Guerrouj, Morocco	Noah Ngeny, Kenya	Noureddine Morceli, Algeria	Hicham El Guerrouj, Morocco	Hicham El Guerrouj, Morocco

CYCLISTS WITH THE MOST TOUR DE FRANCE WINS

Number of first-place finishes

7	5	5	5	5
Lance Armstrong, USA	Eddy Merckx, Belgium	Jacques Anquetil, France	Bernard Hinault, France	Miguel Indurain, Spain

Cyclist with the
MOST TOUR DE FRANCE WINS
Lance Armstrong

LANCE ARMSTRONG was the first cyclist to cross the finish line to win 7 Tour de France races. Armstrong won his first race in 1999, just 3 years after being diagnosed with cancer. He went on to win the top cycling event for the next 6 years, retiring after his 2005 victory. Armstrong has received many awards and honors during his career, including being named *Sports Illustrated*'s "Sportsman of the Year" in 2002. Armstrong also formed the Lance Armstrong Foundation, which supports people recovering from cancer.

7

LPGA Golfer with the
LOWEST SEASONAL AVERAGE

Lorena Ochoa

LORENA OCHOA had the lowest seasonal average in the LPGA in 2007 with 69.69. In fact, that's the fourth-lowest scoring average in LPGA history! Ochoa, who entered the LPGA in 2003, accomplished several other impressive feats in 2006. She won 6 tournaments and was named Rolex Player of the Year. She earned almost $2.6 million, becoming just the second player to pass $2 million in earnings in a single season. During her short career, Ochoa has played in 124 LPGA events and finished in the top three 45 times.

8

LPGA GOLFERS WITH THE LOWEST SEASONAL AVERAGES

Seasonal average in 2007

69.69	70.50	70.86	71.27	71.28
Lorena Ochoa	Paula Creamer	Suzann Pettersen	Annika Sorenstam	Stacy Prammanasudh

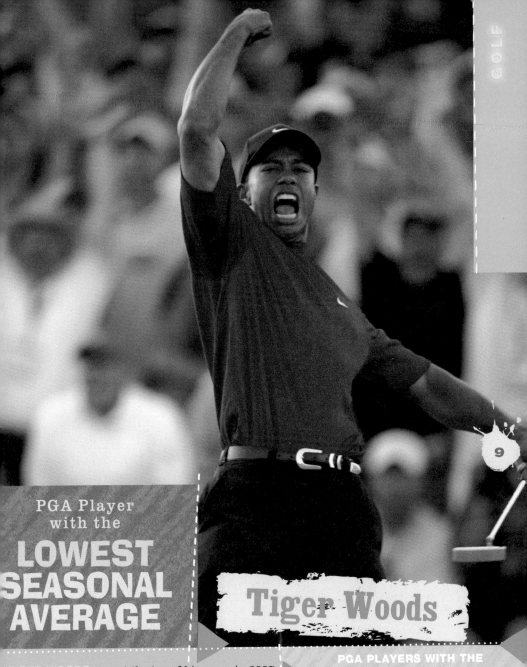

PGA Player with the
LOWEST SEASONAL AVERAGE

Tiger Woods

TIGER WOODS was at the top of his game in 2007 with the lowest PGA seasonal average of 67.79. Woods started his professional golfing career in 1996, and since then he has won more than 64 tournaments. Woods also helped the United States win the World Cup team title in 2000. And at 21 years old, he became the youngest person to complete the career Grand Slam of professional major championships. In 2001, he became the first golfer in history to hold all 4 professional major championships at the same time. Woods's career PGA winnings total more than $79.9 million.

PGA PLAYERS WITH THE LOWEST SEASONAL AVERAGES

Seasonal average in 2007

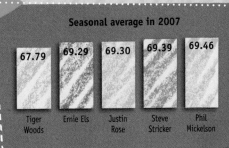

Tiger Woods	Ernie Els	Justin Rose	Steve Stricker	Phil Mickelson
67.79	69.29	69.30	69.39	69.46

10

LPGA's
HIGHEST-PAID GOLFER

Annika Sorenstam

ANNIKA SORENSTAM has earned $21.2 million since her LPGA career began in 1994. During this time, she has had 69 career victories, including 9 majors. In 2005, Sorenstam earned her eighth Rolex Player of the Year award—the most in LPGA history. She also became the first player to sweep Rolex Player of the Year honors, the Vare Trophy, and the ADT Official Money List title 5 times. Sorenstam also earned her fifth consecutive Mizuno Classic title, making her the first golfer in LPGA history to win the same event 5 consecutive years.

LPGA'S HIGHEST-PAID GOLFERS

Career earnings, in millions of US dollars

Annika Sorenstam	Karrie Webb	Juli Inkster	Lorena Ochoa	Se Ri Pak
$21.2	$13.5	$12.0	$10.8	$9.8

GOLFERS WITH THE MOST MAJOR TOURNAMENT WINS

Major tournament wins

Jack Nicklaus, 1962–1986	Tiger Woods, 1997–	Walter Hagen, 1914–1929	Ben Hogan, 1946–1953	Gary Player, 1959–1978
18	13	11	9	9

Golfer with the MOST MAJOR TOURNAMENT WINS

Jack Nicklaus

Golfing great JACK NICKLAUS has won a total of 18 major championships. His wins include 6 Masters, 5 PGAs, 4 US Opens, and 3 British Opens. Nicklaus was named PGA Player of the Year 5 times. He was a member of the winning US Ryder Cup team 6 times and was an individual World Cup winner a record 3 times. He was inducted into the World Golf Hall of Fame in 1974, just 12 years after he turned professional. He joined the US Senior PGA Tour in 1990. In addition to playing the game, Nicklaus has designed close to 200 golf courses and written a number of popular books about the sport.

11

12

Women's Basketball Team with the

MOST NCAA CHAMPION-SHIPS

Tennessee

THE TENNESSEE LADY VOLUNTEERS have won 7 NCAA basketball championships. The Lady Vols won their latest championship in 2007. In 1998 they had a perfect record of 39–0, which was the most seasonal wins ever in women's collegiate basketball. In 2004, Tennessee was in the championship but was beaten by the University of Connecticut Huskies. Since 1976, an impressive 14 Lady Vols have been to the Olympics, and 5 Lady Vols have been inducted into the Women's Basketball Hall of Fame in Knoxville, Tennessee.

WOMEN'S TEAMS WITH THE MOST NCAA CHAMPIONSHIPS

Wins

University of Tennessee	University of Connecticut	Louisiana Tech	Stanford University	University of Southern California
7	5	2	2	2

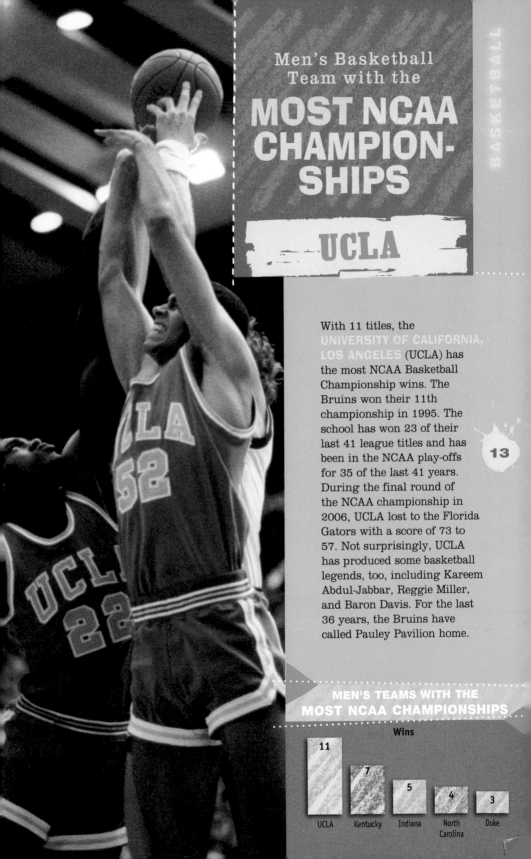

Men's Basketball Team with the

MOST NCAA CHAMPION-SHIPS

UCLA

With 11 titles, the UNIVERSITY OF CALIFORNIA, LOS ANGELES (UCLA) has the most NCAA Basketball Championship wins. The Bruins won their 11th championship in 1995. The school has won 23 of their last 41 league titles and has been in the NCAA play-offs for 35 of the last 41 years. During the final round of the NCAA championship in 2006, UCLA lost to the Florida Gators with a score of 73 to 57. Not surprisingly, UCLA has produced some basketball legends, too, including Kareem Abdul-Jabbar, Reggie Miller, and Baron Davis. For the last 36 years, the Bruins have called Pauley Pavilion home.

13

MEN'S TEAMS WITH THE MOST NCAA CHAMPIONSHIPS

Wins

11	7	5	4	3
UCLA	Kentucky	Indiana	North Carolina	Duke

NBA Team with the
MOST CHAMPION-SHIP TITLES

Boston Celtics

14

The BOSTON CELTICS are the most successful team in the NBA with 16 championship wins. The first win came in 1957, and the team went on to win the next 7 consecutive titles—the longest streak of consecutive championship wins in the history of U.S. sports. The most recent championship title came in 1986. The Celtics entered the Basketball Association of America in 1946, which later merged into the NBA in 1949. The Celtics have made the NBA play-offs for 3 consecutive seasons from 2001 to 2004, but they were eliminated in the first round each time.

NBA TEAMS WITH THE MOST CHAMPIONSHIP TITLES

Number of championship titles

Boston Celtics	Los Angeles Lakers	Chicago Bulls	San Antonio Spurs	Detroit Pistons
16	14	6	4	3

MICHAEL JORDAN

15

NBA Player with the
HIGHEST SCORING AVERAGE

Wilt Chamberlain
& Michael Jordan

Both MICHAEL JORDAN and WILT CHAMBERLAIN averaged an amazing 30.1 points per game during their legendary careers. Jordan played for the Chicago Bulls and the Washington Wizards. He led the league in scoring for 7 years. During the 1986 season, he became only the second person ever to score 3,000 points in a single season. Chamberlain played for the Philadelphia Warriors, the Philadelphia 76ers, and the Los Angeles Lakers. In addition to the highest scoring average, he also holds the record for the most games with 50 or more points, with 118.

PLAYERS WITH THE HIGHEST CAREER SCORING AVERAGES

Average points per game

30.1	30.1	27.8	27.4	27.4
Wilt Chamberlain, 1959–1973	Michael Jordan, 1984–1998; 2001–2003	Allen Iverson, 1996–	Elgin Baylor, 1958–1971	LeBron James, 2003–

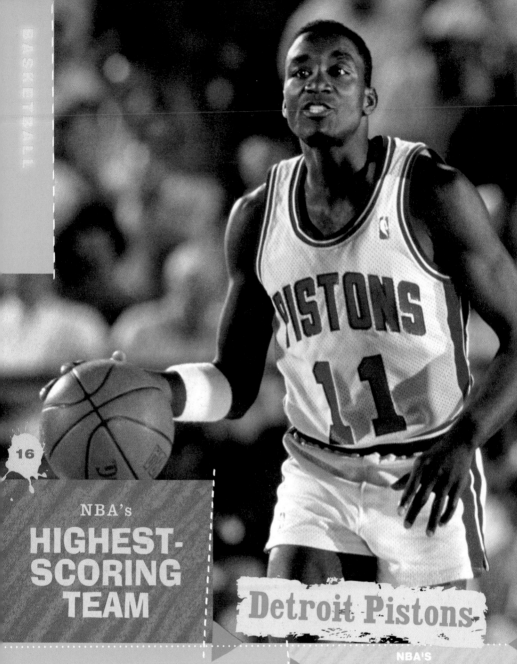

16

Detroit Pistons

On December 13, 1983, the DETROIT PISTONS beat the Denver Nuggets with a score of 186 to 184 at McNichols Arena in Denver, Colorado. The game was tied at 145 at the end of regular play, and 3 overtime periods were needed to determine the winner. During the game, both the Pistons and the Nuggets each had 6 players who scored in the double figures. Four players scored more than 40 points each, which was an NBA first. The Pistons scored 74 field goals that night, claiming another NBA record that still stands today.

NBA'S HIGHEST-SCORING TEAMS

Points scored by a team in one game

186	184	173	173	171
Detroit Pistons, vs. Denver Nuggets, 1983	Denver Nuggets, vs. Detroit Pistons, 1983	Boston Celtics, vs. Minneapolis Lakers, 1959	Phoenix Suns, vs. Denver Nuggets, 1990	San Antonio Spurs, vs. Milwaukee Bucks, 1982

NBA PLAYERS WITH THE HIGHEST SALARIES

Annual salaries, in millions of US dollars

$23.8	$21.7	$20.1	$20.1	$20.0
Kevin Garnett	Michael Finley	Stephon Marbury	Allen Iverson	Shaquille O'Neal

NBA Player with the
HIGHEST SALARY

Kevin Garnett

KEVIN GARNETT earns $23.8 million a season as a forward for the Boston Celtics. Garnett—who stands 1 inch (2.5 cm) shy of 7 feet (2.1 m)—played for the Timberwolves from 1995 to 2007. Since he entered the NBA he has played in more than 900 games with an average of 20.5 points per game. Garnett also tops the league in rebounds, ranking number one in total rebounds (625), rebounds per game (12.5), defensive rebounds (499), and defensive rebounds per game (10).

WNBA Player with the
HIGHEST FREE THROW SCORING AVERAGE

Eva Nemcova

Retired player **EVA NEMCOVA** has a free throw average of .897. Nemcova played for the Cleveland Rockets from 1997 to 2001 and was the fourth overall draft pick during the league's inaugural year. In 2000, she set a WNBA free throw record when she sank 66 consecutive shots that season.

18

WNBA PLAYERS WITH THE HIGHEST FREE THROW SCORING AVERAGES

Career free throw average

.897	.885	.882	.876	.874
Eva Nemcova, 1997–2001	Seimone Augustus, 2006–	Elena Tornikidou, 1999–2001	Sue Bird, 2002–	Becky Hammon, 1999–

19

NBA Player with the
MOST CAREER POINTS

Kareem Abdul-Jabbar

During his highly successful career, KAREEM ABDUL-JABBAR scored a total of 38,387 points. In 1969, Abdul-Jabbar began his NBA tenure with the Milwaukee Bucks. He was named Rookie of the Year in 1970. The following year he scored 2,596 points and helped the Bucks win the NBA championship. He was traded to the Los Angeles Lakers in 1975. With his new team, Abdul-Jabbar won the NBA championship in 1980, 1982, 1985, 1987, and 1988. He retired from basketball in 1989 and was inducted into the Basketball Hall of Fame in 1995.

PLAYERS WITH THE MOST CAREER POINTS

Points scored

38,387	36,928	32,292	31,419	27,409
Kareem Abdul-Jabbar, 1969–1989	Karl Malone, 1985–2004	Michael Jordan, 1984–1998; 2001–2003	Wilt Chamberlain, 1959–1973	Moses Malone, 1974–1994

WNBA Player with the

HIGHEST CAREER PPG AVERAGE

Seimone Augustus

Minnesota Lynx SEIMONE AUGUSTUS leads the WNBA with an average of 22.3 points per game. Augustus was the first overall draft pick in 2006. The 6-foot (1.8-m) guard from Louisiana State was awarded the Naismith Player of the Year Award in 2005, and went on to win the AP Player of the Year Award in 2006. During her first season with the WNBA, Augustus was ranked second in points per game (21.9), field goals made (148), points (744), and field goal attempts (620).

20

WNBA PLAYERS WITH THE HIGHEST CAREER PPG AVERAGES

Average points per game*

22.3	21.0	19.4	19.3	18.3
Seimone Augustus, 2006–	Cynthia Cooper, 1997–2000	Diana Taurasi, 2004–	Lauren Jackson, 2001–	Cappie Poindexter, 2006–

*As of February 11, 2008

WNBA Player
with the

MOST CAREER POINTS

Lisa Leslie

BASKETBALL

Points scored*

5,567	5,048	4,762	4,500	4,412
Lisa Leslie, 1997~	Tina Thompson, 1997~	Katie Smith, 2000~	Sheryl Swoopes, 1997~	Lauren Jackson, 2001~

*As of June 16, 2008

LISA LESLIE—center for the Los Angeles Sparks—has scored 5,567 points in her career. Leslie has a career average of 17.6 points per game. She was named MVP of the WNBA All-Star Games in 1999, 2001, and 2002. Leslie was also a member of the 1996 and 2000 Olympic gold-medal-winning women's basketball teams. In both 2001 and 2002, Leslie led her team to victory in the WNBA championship and was named Finals MVP. Leslie set another record on July 30, 2002, when she became the first player in WNBA history to slam-dunk in a game.

21

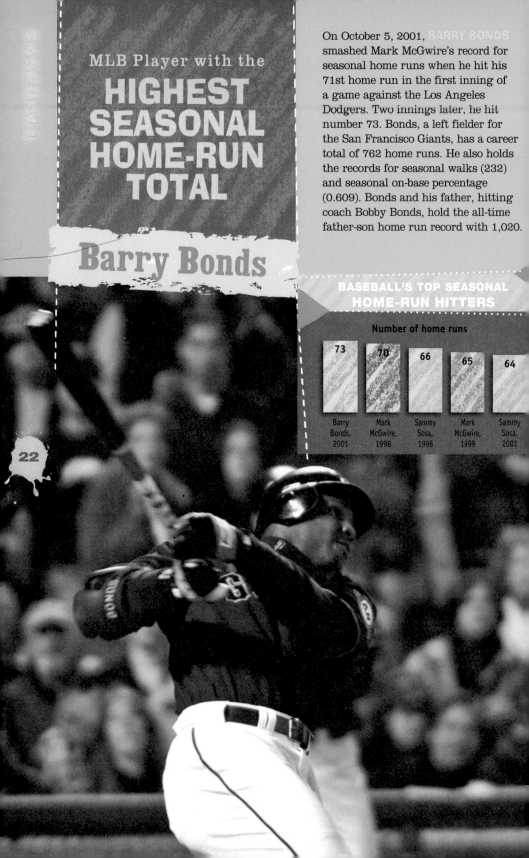

MLB Player with the

HIGHEST SEASONAL HOME-RUN TOTAL

Barry Bonds

On October 5, 2001, BARRY BONDS smashed Mark McGwire's record for seasonal home runs when he hit his 71st home run in the first inning of a game against the Los Angeles Dodgers. Two innings later, he hit number 73. Bonds, a left fielder for the San Francisco Giants, has a career total of 762 home runs. He also holds the records for seasonal walks (232) and seasonal on-base percentage (0.609). Bonds and his father, hitting coach Bobby Bonds, hold the all-time father-son home run record with 1,020.

BASEBALL'S TOP SEASONAL HOME-RUN HITTERS

Number of home runs

73	70	66	65	64
Barry Bonds, 2001	Mark McGwire, 1998	Sammy Sosa, 1998	Mark McGwire, 1999	Sammy Sosa, 2001

22

23

World's
ALL-TIME HOME-RUN HITTER

Barry Bonds

BARRY BONDS has hit more home runs than anyone who ever played in the MLB, cracking 762 balls over the wall during his ongoing career. Bonds has hit more than 30 home runs in a season 13 times—another MLB record. During his impressive career, Bonds has won 8 Gold Gloves, 12 Silver Slugger Awards, and 13 All-Star Awards. Bonds began his career with the Pittsburgh Pirates in 1986; he was later transferred to the San Francisco Giants in 1993 and has played for the team since then. He is only one of 3 players to join the 700 Home Run Club.

WORLD'S ALL-TIME HOME-RUN HITTERS

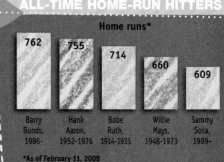

Home runs*

762	755	714	660	609
Barry Bonds, 1986-	Hank Aaron, 1952-1976	Babe Ruth, 1914-1935	Willie Mays, 1948-1973	Sammy Sosa, 1989-

*As of February 11, 2008

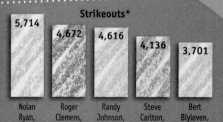

MLB Player
with the
MOST CAREER STRIKE-OUTS

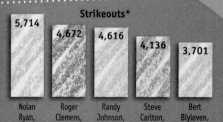

Nolan Ryan

24

NOLAN RYAN leads Major League Baseball with an incredible 5,714 career strikeouts. In his impressive 28-year career, he played for the New York Mets, the California Angels, the Houston Astros, and the Texas Rangers. The right-handed pitcher from Refugio, Texas, led the American League in strikeouts 10 times. In 1989, at the age of 42, Ryan became the oldest pitcher ever to lead the Major Leagues in strikeouts. Ryan set another record in 1991 when he pitched his seventh career no-hitter.

PITCHERS WITH THE MOST CAREER STRIKEOUTS

Strikeouts*

5,714	4,672	4,616	4,136	3,701
Nolan Ryan, 1966–1993	Roger Clemens, 1984–	Randy Johnson, 1989–	Steve Carlton, 1965–1988	Bert Blyleven, 1970–1992

*As of February 11, 2008

25

MLB Player with the MOST CAREER HITS

Pete Rose

PETE ROSE belted an amazing 4,256 hits during his 23 years of professional baseball. He got his record-setting hit in 1985, when he was a player-manager for the Cincinnati Reds. By the time Pete Rose retired as a player from Major League Baseball in 1986, he had set several other career records. Rose holds the Major League records for the most career games (3,562), the most times at bat (14,053), and the most seasons with more than 200 hits (10). During his career, he played for the Cincinnati Reds, the Philadelphia Phillies, and the Montreal Expos.

PLAYERS WITH THE MOST CAREER HITS

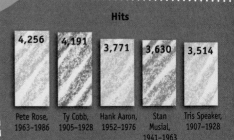

Hits

4,256	4,191	3,771	3,630	3,514
Pete Rose, 1963–1986	Ty Cobb, 1905–1928	Hank Aaron, 1952–1976	Stan Musial, 1941–1963	Tris Speaker, 1907–1928

26

MLB Player with the
MOST EXPENSIVE CONTRACT

Alex Rodriguez

ALEX RODRIGUEZ signed a 10-year deal with the Texas Rangers for $25.7 million in 2001. This does not include any bonuses the shortstop may earn for winning titles or awards, or any money he could make from potential endorsements. The right-hander began his successful career with Seattle in 1994. In 2004, Rodriguez joined the New York Yankees, and the ball club is now responsible for paying the majority of his contract. In 2005, Rodriguez won the American League MVP award.

PLAYERS WITH THE MOST EXPENSIVE CONTRACT

Yearly salary, in millions of US dollars

$25.7	$20.0	$18.9	$18.3	$18.1
Alex Rodriguez, New York Yankees	Manny Ramirez, Boston Red Sox	Derek Jeter, New York Yankees	Carlos Zambrano, Chicago Cubs	Andruw Jones, LA Dodgers

MLB Player with the

MOST CAREER RUNS

Rickey Henderson

Career runs

2,295	2,245	2,227	2,174	2,174
Rickey Henderson, 1979–2003	Ty Cobb, 1905–1928	Barry Bonds, 1986–	Hank Aaron, 1954–1976	Babe Ruth, 1914–1935

During his 25 years in the majors, baseball great RICKEY HENDERSON boasts the most career runs with 2,295. Henderson got his start with the Oakland Athletics in 1979, and went on to play for the Yankees, the Mets, the Mariners, the Red Sox, the Padres, the Dodgers, and the Angels. Henderson won a Gold Glove Award in 1981, and the American League MVP award in 1989 and 1990. Henderson is also known as the "Man of Steal" because he holds the MLB record for most stolen bases in a career with 1,406.

27

JOE DIMAGGIO

Most MVP Awards in the
AMERICAN LEAGUE

Yogi Berra, Joe DiMaggio, Jimmie Foxx, Mickey Mantle, & Alex Rodriguez

With 3 honors each, YOGI BERRA, JOE DIMAGGIO, JIMMIE FOXX, MICKEY MANTLE, and ALEX RODRIGUEZ all hold the record for the Most Valuable Player awards during their professional careers. DiMaggio, Berra, Mantle, and Rodriguez were all New York Yankees. Foxx played for the Athletics, the Cubs, and the Phillies. The player with the biggest gap between wins was DiMaggio, who won his first award in 1939 and his last in 1947. Also nicknamed "Joltin' Joe" and the "Yankee Clipper," DiMaggio began playing in the major leagues in 1936. The following year, he led the league in home runs and runs scored. He was elected to the Baseball Hall of Fame in 1955.

PLAYERS WITH THE MOST AMERICAN LEAGUE MVP AWARDS

Most Valuable Player (MVP) awards

3	3	3	3	3
Yogi Berra, 1946–1963, 1965	Joe DiMaggio, 1936–1951	Jimmie Foxx, 1925–1945	Mickey Mantle, 1951–1968	Alex Rodriguez, 1994–

PLAYERS WITH THE MOST NATIONAL LEAGUE MVP AWARDS

Most MVP Awards in the NATIONAL LEAGUE

Barry Bonds

Most Valuable Player (MVP) awards

Barry Bonds, 1986–	Roy Campanella, 1948–1957	Stan Musial, 1941–1963	Mike Schmidt, 1972–1989	Ernie Banks, 1953–1971
7	3	3	3	2

San Francisco Giant BARRY BONDS has earned 7 Most Valuable Player awards for his amazing achievements in the National Baseball League. He received his first 2 MVP awards in 1990 and 1992 while playing for the Pittsburgh Pirates. The next 5 awards came while wearing the Giants uniform in 1993, 2001, 2002, 2003, and 2004. Bonds is the first player to win an MVP award 3 times in consecutive seasons. In fact, Bonds is the only baseball player in history to have won more than 3 MVP awards.

29

MLB Team with the

MOST WORLD SERIES WINS

New York Yankees

Between 1923 and 2000, the NEW YORK YANKEES were the World Series champions a record 26 times. The team picked up their latest win in October of 2000 when they beat the New York Mets. The Yankees beat the Mets 4 games to 1 to win their third consecutive championship. Since their early days, the team has included some of baseball's greatest players, including Babe Ruth, Lou Gehrig, Yogi Berra, Joe DiMaggio, and Mickey Mantle.

TEAMS WITH THE MOST WORLD SERIES WINS

Wins

26	10	9	7	6
NY Yankees, 1923–2000	St. Louis Cardinals, 1926–2006	Philadelphia/ Kansas City/ Oakland Athletics, 1910–1989	Boston Red Sox, 1903–2007	Brooklyn/ LA Dodgers 1955–1988

30

31

MLB Player with the
MOST CY YOUNG AWARDS

Roger Clemens

ROGER CLEMENS, a starting pitcher for the Houston Astros, has earned a record 7 Cy Young awards during his career so far. He set a Major League record in April 1986 when he struck out 20 batters in one game. He later tied this record in September 1996. In September 2001, Clemens became the first Major League pitcher to win 20 of his first 21 decisions in one season. In June 2003, he became the first pitcher in more than a decade to win his 300th game. He also struck out his 4,000th batter that year.

PITCHERS WITH THE MOST CY YOUNG AWARDS

Cy Young awards

7	5	4	4	3
Roger Clemens, 1984–	Randy Johnson, 1988–	Steve Carlton, 1965–1988	Greg Maddux, 1986–	Sandy Koufax, 1955–1966

MLB Player with the
MOST AT BATS
Pete Rose

PETE ROSE has stood behind the plate for 14,053 at bats—more than any other Major League player. Rose signed with the Cincinnati Reds after graduating high school in 1963 and played second base. During his impressive career, Rose set several other records, including the most singles in the Major Leagues (3,315), most seasons with 600 or more at bats in the major leagues (17), most career doubles in the National League (746), and most career runs in the National League (2,165). He was also named World Series MVP, *Sports Illustrated* Sportsman of the Year, and *The Sporting News* Man of the Year.

PLAYERS WITH THE
MOST AT BATS

At bats

14,053	12,364	11,988	11,551	11,429
Pete Rose	Hank Aaron	Carl Yastrzemski	Cal Ripken, Jr.	Ty Cobb

33

MLB Player with the
MOST CAREER RBIs

Hank Aaron

During his 23 years in the major leagues, right-handed HANK AARON batted in an incredible 2,297 runs. Aaron began his professional career with the Indianapolis Clowns, a team in the Negro American League, in 1952. He was traded to the Milwaukee Braves in 1954 and won the National League batting championship with an average of .328. He was named the league's Most Valuable Player a year later when he led his team to a World Series victory. Aaron retired as a player in 1976 and was inducted into the Baseball Hall of Fame in 1982.

PLAYERS WITH THE MOST CAREER RBIS

Runs batted in

2,297	2,213	2,076	1,996	1,995
Hank Aaron, 1952–1976	Babe Ruth, 1914–1935	Cap Anson, 1876–1897	Barry Bonds, 1986–	Lou Gehrig, 1923–1939

MLB Player Who Played the
MOST CONSECUTIVE GAMES

Cal Ripken, Jr.

Baltimore Oriole CAL RIPKEN, JR., played 2,632 consecutive games from May 30, 1982, to September 20, 1998. The right-handed third baseman also holds the record for the most consecutive innings played: 8,243. In June 1996, Ripken also broke the world record for consecutive games with 2,216, surpassing Sachio Kinugasa of Japan. When he played as a shortstop, Ripken set Major League records for most home runs (345) and most extra base hits (855) for his position. He has started in the All-Star Game a record 19 times in a row.

PLAYERS WITH THE MOST CONSECUTIVE GAMES PLAYED

Consecutive games played

2,632	2,130	1,307	1,207	1,152
Cal Ripken, Jr., 1978–2001	Lou Gehrig, 1923–1939	Everett Scott, 1914–1925	Steve Garvey, 1968–1988	Miguel Tejada, 1997–

34

35

NFL Quarterback with the
MOST PASSING YARDS

Brett Favre

Quarterback BRETT FAVRE knows how to hit his receivers, completing 61,655 passing yards during his amazing career. He has a completion rate of 61.4%, and has connected for 442 touchdowns. Favre is also the NFL's all-time leader in passing touchdowns (425), completions (5,202), and attempts (8,224). And with 153 career wins, he leads all other quarterbacks in game victories too. Favre began his career with the Atlanta Falcons in 1991. He was traded to the Green Bay Packers the next season, and signed a "life" contract with them in 2001.

PLAYERS WITH THE MOST PASSING YARDS

Yards

61,655	61,361	51,475	49,325	47,003
Brett Favre, 1991–	Dan Marino, 1983–2000	John Elway, 1983–1999	Warren Moon, 1984–2000	Fran Tarkenton, 1961–1978

36

NFL Player with the HIGHEST CAREER RUSHING TOTAL

Emmitt Smith

Running back EMMITT SMITH holds the record for all-time rushing yards with 18,355. Smith began his career with the Dallas Cowboys in 1990 and played with the team until the end of the 2002 season. In 2003, Smith signed a 2-year contract with the Arizona Cardinals. Smith also holds the NFL records for the most carries with 4,142 and the most rushing touchdowns with 164. After 15 years in the NFL, Smith retired at the end of the 2004 season.

PLAYERS WITH THE HIGHEST CAREER RUSHING TOTALS

Rushing yards

Emmitt Smith, 1990–2004	Walter Payton, 1975–1987	Barry Sanders, 1989–1999	Curtis Martin, 1995–2007	Jerome Bettis, 1993–2006
18,355	16,726	15,269	14,101	13,662

NFL Player with the
MOST CAREER TOUCH-DOWNS

Jerry Rice

JERRY RICE has scored a record 207 touchdowns. He is widely considered to be one of the greatest wide receivers ever to play in the National Football League. Rice holds a total of 14 NFL records, including career receptions (1,549), receiving yards (22,895), receiving touchdowns (197), consecutive 100-catch seasons (4), most games with 100 receiving yards (73), and many others. He was named NFL Player of the Year twice, *Sports Illustrated* Player of the Year 4 times, and NFL Offensive Player of the Year once. Rice retired from the NFL in 2005.

37

PLAYERS WITH THE MOST CAREER TOUCHDOWNS

Touchdowns scored

207	175	145	136	131
Jerry Rice, 1985–2005	Emmitt Smith, 1990–2004	Marcus Allen, 1982–1996	Marshall Faulk, 1994–2005	Terrell Owens, 1996–

NFL Player with the

MOST SINGLE-SEASON TOUCH-DOWNS

Shaun Alexander

Seattle Seahawks running back **SHAUN ALEXANDER** scored 28 touchdowns in the 2005 season. He had 27 rushing touchdowns and 1 receiving touchdown, and became the first player in NFL history to score 15 or more touchdowns in 5 consecutive seasons. He also led the league in rushing that year with 1,880 yards. For all of these achievements, Alexander was named league MVP in 2005. During his 6-year NFL career, Alexander has scored a total of 100 touchdowns and rushed for 7,817 yards.

PLAYERS WITH THE MOST SINGLE-SEASON TOUCHDOWNS

Touchdowns scored

28	27	26	25	24
Shaun Alexander, 2005	Priest Holmes, 2003	Marshall Faulk, 2000	Emmitt Smith, 1995	John Riggins, 1983

NFL Player with the
HIGHEST CAREER SCORING TOTAL

Morten Andersen

MORTEN ANDERSEN leads the NFL in scoring with a career total of 2,544 points. He has made 565 field goals out of 709 attempts, giving him a 79.9% completion rate. He has scored 849 extra points out of 859 attempts, resulting in a 98.8% success rate. Andersen, a placekicker who began his career in 1982 with the New Orleans Saints, currently plays for the Atlanta Falcons. Known as the Great Dane, partly because of his birthplace of Denmark, Andersen has played 382 professional games. His most successful season was in 1995, when he scored 122 points.

39

PLAYERS WITH THE HIGHEST CAREER SCORING TOTALS

Points scored

Morten Andersen, 1982–2004	Gary Anderson, 1982–2005	George Blanda, 1949–1975	Matt Stover, 1991–	John Carney, 1988–
2,544	2,434	2,002	1,822	1,812

40

NFL Team with the
MOST SUPER BOWL WINS

Cowboys, 49ers, & Steelers

With 5 championships each, the DALLAS COWBOYS, the SAN FRANCISCO 49ERS, and the PITTSBURGH STEELERS all hold the record for the most Super Bowl wins. The first championship win for the Cowboys was in 1972, which was followed by wins in 1978, 1993, 1994, and 1996. Out of those 5 victories, the game with the most spectators was Super Bowl XXVII, when Dallas defeated the Buffalo Bills at the Rose Bowl in Pasadena, California, in 1993. The 49ers had their first win in 1982, and repeated their victory in 1985, 1989, 1990, and 1995.

TEAMS WITH THE MOST SUPER BOWL WINS

Super Bowls won

Dallas Cowboys	San Francisco 49ers	Pittsburgh Steelers	Green Bay Packers	Washington Redskins
5	5	5	3	3

TOP-WINNING NFL COACH

Don Shula

TOP-WINNING NFL COACHES

Games won

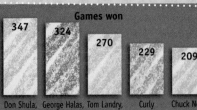

347	324	270	229	209
Don Shula, 1963–1995	George Halas, 1922–1929, 1933–1941, 1946–1955, 1958–1967	Tom Landry, 1960–1988	Curly Lambeau, 1919–1957	Chuck Noel, 1969–1991

DON SHULA led his teams to a remarkable 347 wins during his 33 years as a head coach in the National Football League. When Shula became head coach of the Baltimore Colts in 1963, he became the youngest head coach in football history. He stayed with the team until 1969 and reached the play-offs 4 times. Shula became the head coach for the Miami Dolphins in 1970 and coached them until 1995. During this time, the Dolphins reached the play-offs 20 times and won at least 10 games a season 21 times. After leading them to Super Bowl wins in 1972 and 1973, Shula became one of only 5 coaches to win the championship in back-to-back years.

41

NFL's HIGHEST-PAID PLAYER

Dwight Freeney

Defensive end DWIGHT FREENEY scored a contract with the Indianapolis Colts worth $30.8 million. Freeney was drafted by the Colts in 2002, and set a rookie record for forcing the most fumbles (9). He was also runner-up Defensive Rookie of the Year. He has become the only player in Colts history to have 4 consecutive double-digit sack seasons (2002 to 2005). He also played in the Pro Bowl from 2003 to 2005. Freeney won Super Bowl XLI with the Colts in February 2007. Freeney has a career total of 199 sacks. He has also been awarded Defensive Player of the Week several times in his career.

NFL'S HIGHEST-PAID PLAYERS

Annual salary, in millions of US dollars

Dwight Freeney	Marc Bulger	Leonard Davis	Gaines Adams	Robert Geathers
$30.8	$17.5	$17.0	$15.4	$14.0

43

NFL Team with the
MOST CONSECUTIVE WINS

New England Patriots

The **NEW ENGLAND PATRIOTS** won 18 consecutive games during the 2003 and 2004 seasons. After finishing September 2003 with 2 wins and 2 losses, the team went on to win the next 15 games, including Super Bowl XXXVIII. When the 2004 season began, the team continued its winning streak for the next 6 games. The Patriots finished the season 14-2, and went on to win Super Bowl XXXIX. With this win, the Patriots became the second team in NFL history to win 3 championships in 4 years.

NFL TEAMS WITH THE MOST CONSECUTIVE GAMES WON

Consecutive games won

18	17	16	16	16
New England Patriots, 2003–2004	Chicago Bears, 1933–1934	Chicago Bears, 1941–1942	New England Patriots, 2007–2008	Miami Dolphins, 1983–1984

44

World's
TOP-EARNING FEMALE TENNIS PLAYER

Lindsey Davenport

LINDSEY DAVENPORT has earned $21.9 million in prize money while playing in the Women's Tennis Association (WTA). Davenport turned pro in 1993 and has been the WTA's top player 4 times. She has won 55 WTA singles titles and 37 WTA doubles titles. Her career singles win-loss record is an impressive 741-191, meaning she's won 80% of her matches. She has finished each season as a top-100 ranked player for 15 years.

WORLD'S TOP-EARNING FEMALE TENNIS PLAYERS

Career earnings, in millions of US dollars

$21.9	$21.8	$21.6	$20.1	$19.3
Lindsey Davenport, 1993–	Steffi Graf, 1982–1999	Martina Navratilova, 1975–1994	Martina Hingis, 1994–	Justine Henin, 1999–

WORLD'S TOP-EARNING MALE TENNIS PLAYER

Career earnings, in millions of US dollars

$43.3	$39.0	$31.1	$25.1	$23.9
Pete Sampras, 1990–2003	Roger Federer, 1998–	Andre Agassi, 1986–2006	Boris Becker, 1984–1997	Yevgeny Kafelnikov, 1992–2004

World's TOP-EARNING MALE TENNIS PLAYER

Pete Sampras

PETE SAMPRAS has earned more than $43 million during his 13 years as a professional tennis player. That averages out to about $9,060 a day! In addition to being the top-earning male tennis player of all time, Sampras also holds several other titles. He has been named ATP Player of the Year a record 6 times, he has the most career match wins with 762, and he has been ranked number one for the most weeks with 286. Sampras also ranks fourth in all-time career singles titles with 64. Sampras retired from tennis in 2003, but returned to the game in 2006 when he signed on to play for the World Team Tennis Pro League.

45

Woman with the
MOST GRAND SLAM SINGLES TITLES

Margaret Court Smith

MARGARET COURT SMITH won 24 Grand Slam singles titles between 1960 and 1975. She is the only woman ever to win the French, British, US, and Australian titles during 1 year in both the singles and doubles competitions. She was only the second woman to win all 4 titles in the same year. During her amazing career, she won a total of 66 Grand Slam championships—more than any other woman. Court was the world's top-seeded female player from 1962 to 1965, 1969 to 1970, and 1973. She was inducted into the International Tennis Hall of Fame in 1979.

WOMEN WITH THE MOST GRAND SLAM SINGLES TITLES

Titles won

Margaret Court Smith, 1960–1975	Steffi Graf, 1987–1999	Helen Wills-Moody, 1923–1938	Chris Evert-Lloyd, 1974–1986	Martina Navratilova, 1974–1995
24	22	19	18	18

Man with the
MOST GRAND SLAM SINGLES TITLES

Pete Sampras

With 14 victories, PETE SAMPRAS holds the record for the most Grand Slam male singles titles. He won 2 Australian Opens, 7 Wimbledon titles, and five U.S. Opens between 1990 and 2002. After not winning a major title in 2 years, Sampras won a surprise victory at the 2002 U.S. Open. He was the number 17 seed and beat Andre Agassi in a 3-hour final match. After a 3-year retirement, Sampras began playing for the World Team Tennis Pro League in 2006.

47

MEN WITH THE MOST GRAND SLAM SINGLES TITLES

Titles won

14	12	12	11	11
Pete Sampras, 1990–2002	Roy Emerson, 1961–1967	Roger Federer, 2003–	Bjorn Borg, 1974–1981	Rod Laver, 1960–1969

TOP FEMALE WORLD-CHAMPION FIGURE SKATERS

Carol Heiss & Michelle Kwan

CAROL HEISS and MICHELLE KWAN—two of America's most successful figure skaters—have each won the Women's World Figure Skating Championships 5 times. Heiss, whose wins came between 1956 and 1960, also won an Olympic silver medal for women's figure skating in 1956, and then a gold medal during the 1960 Winter Olympics in Squaw Valley, California. Kwan won the World Championships in 1996, 1998, 2000, 2001, and 2003. Kwan has also won the Women's U.S. Championships a record 6 times. She picked up a silver medal in the 1998 Olympics and won a bronze in 2002. Kwan went to compete in the 2006 Winter Games, but she had to pull out of the competition when—after qualifying—a groin injury prevented her from continuing.

WOMEN WITH THE MOST WORLD FIGURE-SKATING CHAMPIONSHIP WIN

World Championship wins

5	5	4	3	3
Carol Heiss, USA, 1956–1960	Michelle Kwan, USA, 1996–2003	Katarina Witt, E. Germany, 1984–1988	Sjoukje Dijkstra, Netherlands, 1962–1964	Peggy Fleming, USA, 1966–196

48

MICHELLE KWAN

TOP MALE WORLD-CHAMPION FIGURE SKATERS

Kurt Browning, Scott Hamilton, Hayes Jenkins, & Alexei Yagudin

Figure skaters KURT BROWNING, SCOTT HAMILTON, HAYES JENKINS, and ALEXEI YAGUDIN have each won 4 world championship competitions. Yagudin is from Russia and won his World Championship titles in 1998, 2000, 2001, and 2002. In the 2001–2002 season, Yagudin became the first male skater to win a gold medal in the 4 major skating events— Europeans, Grand Prix Final, Worlds, and the Olympics—in the same year. Yagudin retired in 2003 due to a hip disorder. Browning is from Canada and was inducted into the Canadian Sports Hall of Fame in 1994. Hamilton and Jenkins are from the United States. Hamilton won the competitions from 1981 to 1984. He also won a gold medal in the 1984 Olympics. Jenkins's impressive skating career included winning every major championship between 1953 and 1956.

49

MEN WITH THE MOST WORLD FIGURE-SKATING CHAMPIONSHIP WINS

World Championship wins

4	4	4	4	3
Kurt Browning, Canada, 1989–1993	Scott Hamilton, USA, 1981-1984	Hayes Jenkins, USA, 1953–1956	Alexei Yagudin, Russia, 1988–2002	Yevgeny Plushchenko, Russia, 2001–2004

ALEXEI YAGUDIN

Woman with the
MOST SKIING WORLD CUP TITLES

Annemarie Moser-Proll

Austrian skier ANNEMARIE MOSER-PROLL has won 17 alpine skiing world cup titles during her amazing career. Her wins include 6 in overall competition, another 7 in downhill competition, an additional 3 in giant slalom, and 1 in combined competition. Moser-Proll holds the record for World Cup Championships with 6 wins, and she also holds the record for World Cup races won with 59. Moser-Proll was also successful in Olympic competition. She won downhill and slalom silver medals in 1972, and a gold medal in the downhill in 1980.

50

WOMEN WITH THE MOST ALPINE SKIING WORLD CUP TITLES

Total number of titles won

17	14	11	11	9
Annemarie Moser-Proll, Austria	Vreni Schneider, Switzerland	Renate Götschl, Austria	Katja Seizinger, Germany	Erika Hess, Switzerland

51

Ingemar
Stenmark

Man with the
MOST SKIING WORLD CUP TITLES

Ingemar Stenmark

INGEMAR STENMARK is one of the most successful skiers in the world and has won 19 World Cup titles in alpine skiing. Stenmark won 3 titles in the overall competition, another 8 in the giant slalom, and 8 in the slalom. He also completed 4 of the top 10 most successful seasons in giant slalom in history. In Olympic competition, Stenmark won a bronze medal in 1976 for giant slalom, and gold each for the slalom and giant slalom in 1980. When he retired in 1989, he had won a total of 86 World Cup races.

MEN WITH THE MOST ALPINE SKIING WORLD CUP TITLES

Total number of titles won

19	15	15	14	9
Ingemar Stenmark, Sweden	Marc Girardelli, Luxembourg	Pirmin Zurbriggen, Switzerland	Hermann Maier, Austria	Phil Mahre, USA

52

Rider with the
MOST SUPERBIKE RACE WINS

Carl Fogarty

UK driver CARL FOGARTY won 59 Superbike races during his career. Known by the nickname "Foggy" to his fans, Fogarty won the World Superbike Championship in 1994, 1995, 1998, and 1999. As part of the Ducati racing team, Fogarty set a lap record at the Isle of Man TT Race after he clocked 18 minutes and 18 seconds on a Yamaha 750cc in 1992. He also competed in the 1995 Daytona 200 and finished second. Fogarty retired from racing in 2000.

RIDERS WITH THE MOST SUPERBIKE RACE WINS

Total race wins

59	31	31	27	23
Carl Fogarty, UK	Troy Corser, Australia	Colin Edwards, USA	Doug Polen, USA	Raymand Roche, France

Rider with the
MOST MOTO-CROSS WORLD TITLES

Stefan Everts

STEFAN EVERTS is the king of Motocross with a total of 10 World titles. He won twice on a 500cc bike, 7 more times on a 250cc bike, and once on a 125cc bike. During his 18-year career, he won 101 Grand Prix victories. Everts was named Belgium Sportsman of the Year 5 times. He retired after his final World victory in 2006 and is a consultant and coach for the riders who compete for the KTM racing team.

53

RIDERS WITH THE MOST MOTOCROSS WORLD TITLES

Total FIM wins

Rider	Wins
Stefan Everts, Belgium	10
Joel Robert, Belgium	6
Roger de Coster, Belgium	5
Eric Geboers, Belgium	5
Georges Jobe, Belgium	5

Skateboarders with the MOST X-GAME GOLD MEDALS

Tony Hawk

American TONY HAWK has won 10 gold medals in the Extreme Games for skateboarding between 1995 and 2002. All his medals have come in vertical competition, meaning that the riders compete on a vert ramp similar to a half pipe. Hawk is most famous for nailing the 900—completing 2.5 rotations in the air before landing back on the ramp. He has also invented many skateboarding tricks, including the McHawk, the Madonna, and the Stalefish. Although Hawk is retired from professional skateboarding, he is still active in several businesses including video game consulting, film production, and clothing design.

SKATEBOARDERS WITH THE MOST X-GAME GOLD MEDALS

Total gold medals won

Tony Hawk, USA	Andy Macdonald, USA	Bucky Lasek, USA	Rodil de Araujo, Jr., Brazil	Bob Burnquist, Brazil
10	8	6	5	4

54

55

Athlete with the
MOST X-GAME MEDALS

Dave Mirra

DAVE MIRRA has won 20 medals—14 gold, 4 silver, and 2 bronze—in X-Game competition. He has medaled in every X-Game since he entered the games in 1995. All of Mirra's medals have come in BMX competition, where he performs tricks such as double-backflips, frontflips, triple tailwhips, and backflip drop-ins. In 2006, Mirra formed his own bike company named MirraCo, and competes for the company with other top BMX riders. This same year also marked Mirra's first absence from the X-Games because of injury.

ATHLETES WITH THE MOST X-GAME MEDALS

Total medals won

20	16	15	14	13
Dave Mirra, USA	Andy Macdonald, USA	Tony Hawk, USA	Shaun White, USA	Bob Burnquist, USA

56

Snowboarder with the

MOST CHAMPIONSHIP MEDALS

Nicolas Huet

NICOLAS HUET has won 5 Championship medals while competing as a snowboarder with the Fédération Internationale de Ski (FIS). Huet's medals include 2 golds, 1 silver, and 2 bronzes. Huet's first medal came in 1999 when he won gold in Germany, and his most recent medals came in 2005 when he won a silver and a bronze in Canada. His medals were earned on the parallel slalom and the parallel giant slalom. Nicknamed Nico, Huet spends his time golfing and surfing when he's not on the slopes.

SNOWBOARDERS WITH THE MOST WORLD CHAMPIONSHIP MEDAL

Total of gold, silver, and bronze medals

5	4	3	3	3
Nicolas Huet, France	Antti Autti, Finland	Jasey-Jay Anderson, Canada	Mike Jacoby, USA	Helmut Pramstaller, Austria

Women's Soccer Team with the

MOST WORLD CUP POINTS

USA

Total World Cup points

14	12	5	4	3
USA	Germany	Sweden	Norway	China

The USA Women's Soccer team has accumulated 14 points during World Cup competition. The Fédération Internationale de Football Association (FIFA) awards 4 points for a win, 3 points for runner up, 2 points for third place, and 1 point for fourth. The United States won the Cup in 1991 and 1999. They came in third place in 1995, 2003, and 2007. Some of the star players on the US team at the time of these wins include Mia Hamm, Julie Foudy, Brandi Chastain, Kristine Lilly, and Briana Scurry.

57

58

Man with the
MOST CAPS

Mohamed Al-Deayea

Saudi Arabian soccer great MOHAMED AL-DEAYEA has the most CAPS, or international games, with 181. Al-Deayea began his professional career as a goalie with the Saudi team Al-Ta'ee in 1991 and played there for 9 years. In 2000, he became a member of Al-Hilal and the team's captain. While playing as a part of the Saudi National Team, Al-Deayea reached the World Cup 3 times between 1994 and 2002. He was placed on the 2006 World Cup team but did not play in any games. At the end of the competition, Al-Deayea announced his retirement.

MEN WITH THE
MOST CAPS

Total international games played

181	178	170	164	164
Mohamed Al-Deayea, Saudi Arabia, 1990–2006	Claudio Suárez, Mexico, 1992–	Hossam Hassan, Egypt, 1985–	Adnan Khamées Al-Talyani, UAE, 1984–1997	Cobi Jones, United States, 1992–2007

Country with the
MOST WORLD CUP POINTS

Germany

GERMANY has accumulated a total of 31 points during World Cup soccer competition. A win is worth 4 points, runner-up is worth 3 points, third place is worth 2 points, and fourth place is worth 1 point. Germany has won the World Cup 4 times between 1954 and 1990. Most recently, Germany earned 2 points for a third-place finish in 2006. The World Cup is organized by the Fédération Internationale de Football Association (FIFA) and is played every 4 years.

59

COUNTRIES WITH THE MOST WORLD CUP POINTS

Total points

31	30	25	14	10
Germany/ W. Germany, 1954–2006	Brazil, 1958–2002	Italy, 1934–2006	Argentina, 1978–1986	Uruguay, 1930–1950

Soccer Player with the
HIGHEST SALARY

Ronaldinho

Soccer star RONALDINHO earned $29.5 million in 2007. The midfielder was named the FIFA World Player of the Year in 2004 and 2005. He was also awarded the European Footballer of the Year in 2005, and the FIFPro World Player of the Year in 2005 and 2006. During his career, Ronaldinho has appeared in 280 games and scored 126 goals. Ronaldinho began his career with Grêmio Foot-Ball Porto Alegrense (Grêmio) in 1998, moved to Paris Saint-Germain Football Club (PSG) in 2001, and ended up at FC Barcelona in 2003. He is under contract with the club until 2010.

60

SOCCER PLAYERS WITH THE HIGHEST SALARIES

Annual salary, in millions of US dollars

$29.5	$29.1	$23.4	$17.2	$16.8
Ronaldinho, FC Barcelona	David Beckham, Galaxy	Cristiano Ronaldo, Real Madrid	Wayne Rooney, Manchester United	Michael Ballack, Chelsea

WOMEN WITH THE MOST CAPS

Career CAPS

340	275	271	239	204
Kristine Lilly, USA, 1987–	Mia Hamm, USA, 1987–2004	Julie Foudy, USA, 1988–2004	Joy Fawcett, USA, 1987–2004	Tiffeny Milbrett, USA, 1991–2005

Woman with the MOST CAPS

Kristine Lilly

With a total of 340, KRISTINE LILLY holds the world record for the most CAPS, or international games played. This is the highest number of CAPS in both the men's and women's international soccer organizations. Lilly has played more than 23,500 minutes—that's 392 hours—for the US National Team. In 2004, Lilly scored her 100th international goal, becoming only 1 of 5 women to ever accomplish that. In 2005, Lilly was named US Soccer's Female Athlete of the Year.

61

NHL Team with the
MOST STANLEY CUP WINS

Montreal Canadiens

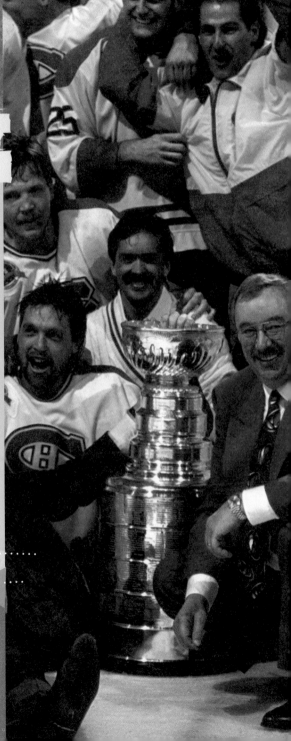

The **MONTREAL CANADIENS** have won an amazing 24 Stanley Cup victories between 1916 and 1993. That's almost one-quarter of all the Stanley Cups ever played. The team plays at Montreal's Molson Centre. The Canadiens were created in December 1909 by J. Ambrose O'Brien to play for the National Hockey Association (NHA). They eventually made the transition into the National Hockey League. Over the years, the Canadiens have included such great players as Maurice Richard, George Hainsworth, Jacques Lemaire, Saku Koivu, and Emile Bouchard.

62

TEAMS WITH THE MOST STANLEY CUP WINS

Stanley Cups won

24				
	11	**10**		
			5	**5**
Montreal Canadiens, 1916–1993	Toronto Maple Leafs, 1932–1967	Detroit Red Wings, 1936–2002	Boston Bruins, 1929–1972	Edmonton Oilers, 1984–1990

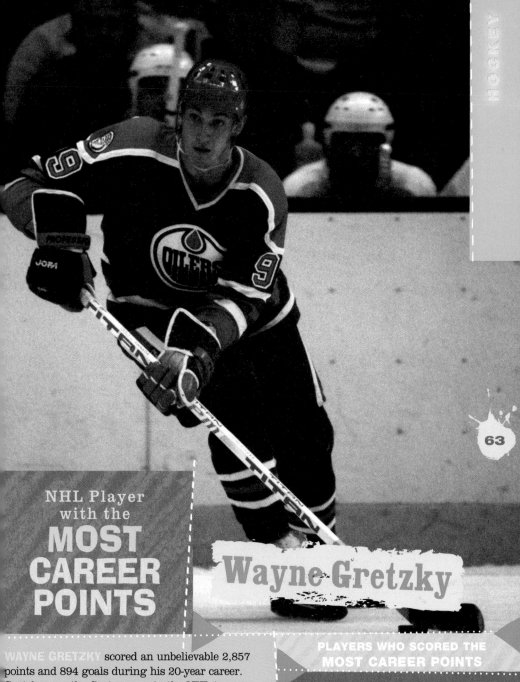

NHL Player with the

MOST CAREER POINTS

Wayne Gretzky

WAYNE GRETZKY scored an unbelievable 2,857 points and 894 goals during his 20-year career. Gretzky was the first person in the NHL to average more than 2 points per game. Many people consider Canadian-born Gretzky to be the greatest player in the history of the National Hockey League. In fact, he is called the "Great One." He officially retired from the sport in 1999 and was inducted into the Hockey Hall of Fame that same year. After his final game, the NHL retired his jersey number (99). In 2005, Gretzky became the head coach of the Phoenix Coyotes.

PLAYERS WHO SCORED THE MOST CAREER POINTS

Points scored

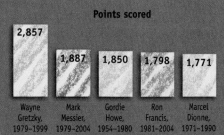

2,857	1,887	1,850	1,798	1,771
Wayne Gretzky, 1979–1999	Mark Messier, 1979–2004	Gordie Howe, 1954–1980	Ron Francis, 1981–2004	Marcel Dionne, 1971–1990

64

NHL Goalie with the
MOST CAREER WINS

Patrick Roy

During his 20 years in the NHL, PATRICK ROY won 551 games. Roy also holds the NHL records for most 30-or-more win seasons (11), most playoff games played (240), most play-off minutes played (14,783), and most play-off wins (148). He was also a member of the Montreal Canadiens when they won the Stanley Cup in 1986 and 1993. Roy helped his team—the Colorado Avalanche—to win the Stanley Cup Championships in 1996 and 2001. On May 29, 2003, Roy announced his retirement from the sport.

GOALTENDERS WITH THE MOST CAREER WINS

Games won

551	534	484	447	437
Patrick Roy, 1984–2003	Martin Brodeur, 1991–	Ed Belfour, 1988–	Terry Sawchuck, 1945–1970	Jacques Plante, 1951–197

World's
MOST VALUABLE HOCKEY TEAM

Toronto Maple Leafs

The TORONTO MAPLE LEAFS are worth an astounding $413 million, making them the most valuable hockey team in the world. This value is determined by assigning a monetary value to each of the team's players, based on their skills, performance, and contract value. Formerly known as the Toronto Arenas, the team was formed in 1917. Ten years later, the team changed to its current name. The Leafs have won 13 Stanley Cups between 1918 and 1967. Some of the most famous players associated with the team include Turk Broda, Tim Horton, Syl Apps, Darryl Sittler, and Ed Belfour. The team's home ice is at the Air Canada Centre.

65

WORLD'S MOST VALUABLE HOCKEY TEAMS

Team value, in millions of US dollars

Toronto Maple Leafs	New York Rangers	Detroit Red Wings	Montreal Canadiens	Dallas Stars
$413	$365	$293	$283	$254

Driver with the
FASTEST DAYTONA 500 WIN

Buddy Baker

Race car legend BUDDY BAKER dominated the competition at the 1980 Daytona 500 with a top average speed of 177 miles (285 km) per hour. It was the first Daytona 500 race run under 3 hours. Baker had a history of speed before this race—he became the first driver to race more than 200 miles (322 km) per hour on a closed course in 1970. During his amazing career, Baker competed in 688 Winston Cup races—he won 19 of them and finished in the top 5 in 198 others. He also won more than $3.6 million. He was inducted into the International Motorsports Hall of Fame in 1997.

66

DRIVERS WITH THE FASTEST DAYTONA 500 WINS

Average speed, in miles (kilometers) per hour

177.60 (285.82)	176.26 (283.66)	172.71 (277.95)	172.26 (277.23)	169.65 (273.03)
Buddy Baker, 1980	Bill Elliott, 1987	Dale Earnhardt, 1998	Bill Elliott, 1985	Richard Petty, 1981

67

Driver with the
FASTEST INDIANAPOLIS 500 WIN

Arie Luyendyk

In 1990, race car driver ARIE LUYENDYK won the Indianapolis 500 with an average speed of 186 miles (299 km) per hour—the fastest average speed ever recorded in the history of the race. This was the first Indy 500 race for Luyendyk, and he drove a Lola/Chevy Indy V8 as part of the Shierson Racing team. In 1997, Luyendyk had another Indy 500 victory with an average speed of 146 miles (235 km) per hour. He also holds the record for the fastest Indy 500 practice lap at a speed of 239 miles (385 km) per hour.

DRIVERS WITH THE FASTEST INDIANAPOLIS 500 WINS

Average speed, in miles (kilometers) per hour

185.98 (299.30)	176.45 (283.98)	170.72 (274.75)	167.61 (269.73)	167.58 (269.73)
Arie Luyendyk, 1990	Rick Mears, 1991	Bobby Rahal, 1986	Juan-Pablo Montoya, 2000	Emerson Fittipaldi, 1989

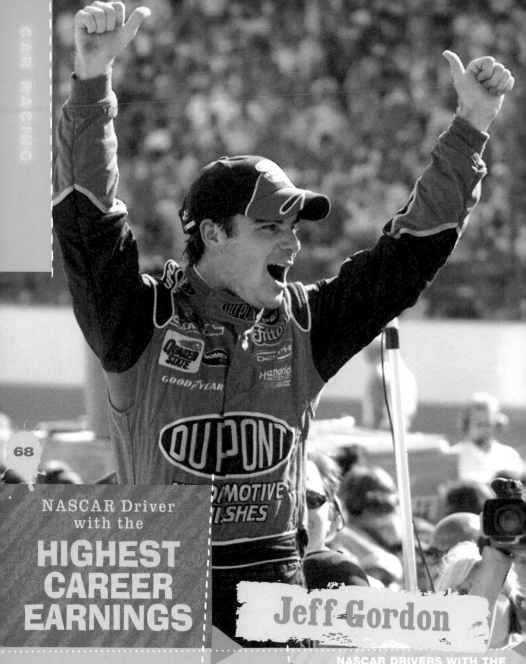

68

NASCAR Driver with the
HIGHEST CAREER EARNINGS

Jeff Gordon

JEFF GORDON has earned more than $93 million since he began racing in 1991. In fact, he was the first driver in history to earn more than $50 million. To date, Gordon has won 4 Winston Cup titles, 3 Daytona 500 titles, and 73 NASCAR Cup victories. His first Daytona 500 win in 1997 came when he was just 25 years old, making him the race's youngest winner. Gordon has 81 career NASCAR victories, placing him sixth on the all-time wins list. He has raced for Hendrick Motorsports since 1992, and is part owner in the business.

NASCAR DRIVERS WITH THE HIGHEST CAREER EARNINGS

Career earnings, in millions of US dollars

Jeff Gordon	Dale Jarrett	Jimmie Johnson	Mark Martin	Rusty Wallace
$93.3	$59.7	$59.5	$53.9	$49.7

Human-Made Records

Transportation

Constructions

Travel

Country
with the

MOST VEHICLES

United States

With more than 238 million vehicles registered in the UNITED STATES, America outnumbers every country in the world in vehicle ownership. There are 136.5 million passenger cars and 101.7 million commercial vehicles in the country. This means that for every two Americans there is one car. That figure doesn't even include all of the trucks, campers, and motorcycles in the country. More than 90% of all US residents have access to motor vehicles. With 19.6 million cars, California is the state with the most registered automobiles in the nation. The average American driver spends about 21 hours each year stuck in traffic.

70

COUNTRIES WITH THE MOST VEHICLES

Number of vehicles, in millions

238.2	76.3	48.3	37.7	35.3
USA	Japan	Germany	Italy	France

Times Sq-42 St Station
Ⓢ Ⓝ Ⓠ Ⓡ Ⓦ
① ② ③ ⑦
♿ Elevator to Ⓝ Ⓠ Ⓡ Ⓦ at 42 St
For Ⓐ Ⓒ Ⓔ enter at 8 Avenue

Enter with or buy MetroCard
6am-12 midnight or see
agent at 42 St & 7 Av

71

City with the World's LONGEST SUBWAY SYSTEM

New York City

The NEW YORK subway system consists of 660 miles (1062.2 km) of track—more than enough to run from the Big Apple to Louisville, Kentucky. An additional 182 miles (292.9 km) of track lie beneath the city streets, but they are not currently in use. New York City has 468 subway stations, which is just 35 fewer than the total number of subway stations throughout the entire country. There are approximately 6,200 subway cars in use, and together they travel about 353.7 million miles (569.2 million km) annually. The New York City subway system opened in 1904 with 9 miles (14.5 km) of track and charged just 5 cents per ride.

CITIES WITH THE WORLD'S LONGEST SUBWAY SYSTEMS

Subway length, in miles (kilometers)

New York	London	Moscow	Tokyo	Paris
660 (410)	253 (157)	178 (111)	174 (108)	134 (83)

72

City with the
BUSIEST SUBWAY SYSTEM

Tokyo

Every year, more than 2.8 million riders pack into the TOKYO subway. The system operates more than 2,500 cars and 282 subway stations. The tracks run for more than 182 miles (292.9 km). The Tokyo Underground Railroad opened in 1927. It has expanded through the years to include 8 subway lines that connect the bustling areas of Chiyoda, Minato, and Chuo. The Tokyo Metro has recently taken steps to upgrade its cars and stations, reinforcing car frames and redesigning station platforms.

WORLD'S BUSIEST SUBWAY SYSTEMS

Passengers per year, in billions

Tokyo	Moscow	New York City	Seoul	Mexico City
2.86	2.61	1.49	1.47	1.44

Country
with the

MOST
ROODS

United States

The UNITED STATES is connected by a system of roads that measures 3,995,186 miles (6,430,366 km). Approximately 2.8 million miles (4.5 million km) of these roads are paved. Some 46,608 miles (75,008 km) of these roads are part of the country's expressways. Americans spend about 100 hours a year driving to work. Because Americans are always on the move, it's not surprising that the nation's highways are frequently tied up with traffic jams. Americans waste about 5.7 billion hours annually because they are stuck in traffic.

73

COUNTRIES WITH THE MOST ROADS

Miles (kilometers) of roads

USA	India	China	Brazil	Japan
3,995,186 (6,430,366)	2,102,072 (3,383,344)	1,162,241 (1,870,661)	1,088,435 (1,751,868)	735,082 (1,183,000)

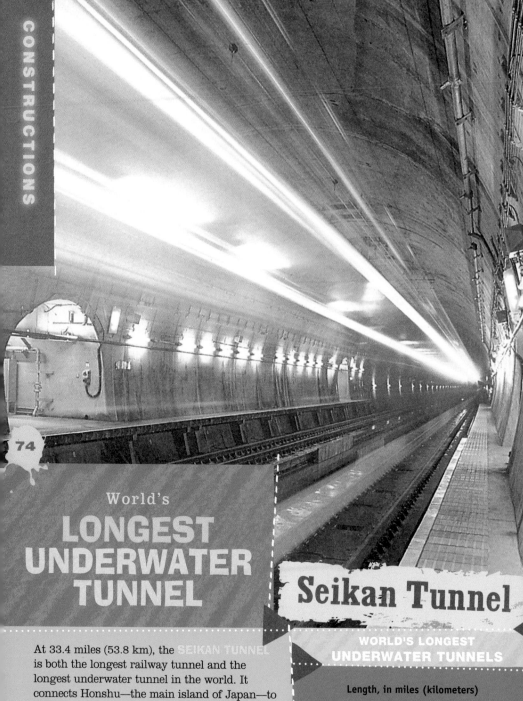

74

World's
LONGEST UNDERWATER TUNNEL

Seikan Tunnel

At 33.4 miles (53.8 km), the SEIKAN TUNNEL is both the longest railway tunnel and the longest underwater tunnel in the world. It connects Honshu—the main island of Japan—to Hokkaido, an island to the north. Some 14.3 miles (23 km) of the tunnel run under the Tsugaru Strait, which connects the Pacific Ocean to the Sea of Japan. A railway in the tunnel transports passengers. Construction began in 1964 and took 24 years to complete at a cost of $7 billion. Today, the Seikan Tunnel is no longer the quickest way between the two islands. Air travel is faster and almost the same price.

WORLD'S LONGEST UNDERWATER TUNNELS

Length, in miles (kilometers)

Seikan Tunnel, Japan	Channel Tunnel, France/England	Lotschberg Base, Switzerland	Guadarrama, Spain	Dai-Shimizu Tunnel, Japan
33.4 (53.8)	31.0 (49.9)	21.0 (33.8)	17.6 (28.3)	13.8 (22.2)

World's
LONGEST ROAD TUNNEL

Laerdal

Length, in miles (kilometers)

Length, in miles (kilometers)				
15.2 (24.5)	11.2 (18.0)	10.3 (16.4)	8.7 (14.0)	8.0 (12.9)
Laerdal Tunnel, Norway	Zhongnanshan, China	St. Gotthard Tunnel, Switzerland	Arlberg Tunnel, Austria	Frejus Tunnel, France/Italy

The LAERDAL TUNNEL was officially opened in Norway on November 27, 2000, and measures 15.2 miles (24.5 km). This huge construction makes its way under large mountain chains to connect the capital, Oslo, to the port of Bergen, Norway's second-largest city. The tunnel is 29.5 feet (9 m) wide and 21 feet (6.3 m) high. It is estimated that about 1,000 cars and trucks make the 20-minute drive through the tunnel each day. To help make the tunnel safe, the designers installed special lighting to keep drivers alert. There are also turning areas in case drivers need to stop. The tunnels are equipped with state-of-the-art ventilation systems and special signal boosters that allow cell phone reception.

World's
HIGHEST CITY

Wenchuan, China

Sitting 16,730 feet (5,099 m) above the sea, WENCHUAN, CHINA, is the world's highest city. That's 3.2 miles (5.2 km) high, more than half the height of Mt. Everest. There are several ancient villages in the area with houses dating back hundreds of years. Located nearby is the Wolong Panda Preserve—one of the last places on Earth where the endangered bears are studied and bred. The city is part of the Sichuan Province, which is located in southwest China. The province covers 207,340 square miles (537,000 sq km) and has a population of 87.2 million.

76

WORLD'S HIGHEST CITIES

Height above sea level, in feet (meters)

16,730 (5,099)	13,045 (3,976)	12,146 (3,702)	12,087 (3,684)	11,916 (3,632)
Wenchuan, China	Potosi, Bolivia	Oruro, Bolivia	Lhasa, Tibet	La Paz, Bolivia

World's
LONGEST SHIP CANAL

Grand Canal

The GRAND CANAL flows for 1,114 miles (1,793 km) through China, connecting Beijing to Hangzhou. The canal measures between 100 and 200 feet (30 and 60 m) wide and between 2 and 15 feet (0.6 and 4.6 m) deep. There are 24 locks and 60 bridges along the Grand Canal. Construction on the canal began in the sixth century BC and continued for 2,000 years. Since most of China's main rivers flow from west to east, the north-and-south flowing canal is an important connection between the Yangtze River valley and the Yellow River valley.

WORLD'S LONGEST SHIP CANALS

Length, in miles (kilometers)

Grand Canal, China	Erie Canal, USA	Gota Canal, Sweden	St. Lawrence Canal, Canada/USA	Canal du Midi, France
1,114 (1,793)	363 (584)	240 (386)	180 (290)	149 (240)

CONSTRUCTIONS

World's
LARGEST MALL

South China Mall

The SOUTH CHINA MALL in Dongguan City is a shopper's paradise with 7.1 million square feet (0.66 million sq m) of retail and entertainment space. There are 11 large department stores, and 1,500 smaller shops. The megamall—which opened in 2005—was designed with seven major areas that resemble Amsterdam, Paris, Rome, Venice, Egypt, the Caribbean, and California. And, for shoppers too tired to walk from one end of the giant retail outlet to the other, there are gondolas and water taxis located on the one-mile, human-made canal that circles the perimeter. Approximately 10,000 people visit the mall each day.

WORLD'S LARGEST MALLS

Area, in millions of square feet (square meters)

7.1 (0.66)	6.0 (0.56)	4.2 (0.39)	3.8 (0.35)	3.6 (0.33)
South China Mall, China	Golden Resources Shopping Mall, China	SM Mall of Asia, Philippines	West Edmonton Mall, Canada	SM Mega-mall, Philippines

79

Amusement Park with the
MOST RIDES

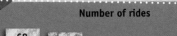
Cedar Point

Located in Sandusky, Ohio, CEDAR POINT offers park visitors 68 rides to enjoy. Skyhawk—the park's newest ride—thrusts riders 125 feet (38 m) into the air and is the largest swing ride in the world. Top Thrill Dragster roller coaster is the tallest in the world at 420 feet (128 m). And with 17 roller coasters, Cedar Point also has the most coasters of any theme park in the world. Over 53,963 feet (16,448 m) of coaster track—more than 10 miles (16.1 km)—run through the park. Cedar Point opened in 1870 and is the second-oldest amusement park in the country.

AMUSEMENT PARKS WITH THE MOST RIDES

Number of rides

68	67	49	44	40
Cedar Point, Ohio, USA	Hersheypark, Pennsylvania, USA	Six Flags Great Adventure, New Jersey, USA	Disneyland, California, USA	Legoland, California, USA

City with the

MOST SKY-SCRAPERS

Hong Kong

A total of 195 skyscrapers rise high above the streets of HONG KONG. In fact, the world's fifth-tallest building—Two International Finance Centre—towers 1,362 feet (415 m) above the city. Because this bustling Chinese business center has only about 160 square miles (414 sq km) of land suitable for building, architects have to build up instead of out. And Hong Kong keeps growing—60 of the city's giant buildings were constructed in the last seven years. Some large development projects, such as the Sky Tower Apartment Complex, added seven skyscrapers to the landscape in just one year.

80

CITIES WITH THE MOST SKYSCRAPERS

Number of skyscrapers

195	186	87	72	65
Hong Kong, China	New York City, New York, USA	Chicago, Illinois, USA	Shanghai, China	Tokyo, Japan

81

World's
TALLEST APARTMENT BUILDING

Q1

Q1, a new luxury apartment complex on Australia's Gold Coast, rises 1,058 feet (323 m) above the surrounding sand. There are 526 apartments within the building's 80 floors. Some apartments have glass-enclosed balconies. Q1 residents can enjoy Australia's only beachside observation deck and a 10-story sky garden. Some other amenities include retail outlets, a lagoon swimming pool, spa, sauna, and fitness center. And just in case all nine elevators are out of order, there are 1,430 steps from the penthouse to the basement.

WORLD'S TALLEST APARTMENT BUILDINGS

Height, in feet (meters)

1,058 (323)	975 (297)	883 (269)	863 (263)	656 (200)
Q1, Gold Coast, Australia	Eureka Tower, Melbourne, Australia	21st Century Tower, UAE	Trump World Towers, New York, USA	Tregunter Tower III, Hong Kong, China

82

World's
LARGEST
DOME

02

The 02 has a roof that measures 1,050 feet (320 m) in diameter and covers 861,113 square feet (80,000 sq m). That's large enough to contain the Great Pyramid of Giza! The roof is made of 107,639 square feet (10,000 sq m) of fabric and is held up by 43 miles of steel cable. It also boasts a movie complex, theaters, and restaurants. The dome was built for the country's millennium celebration. After the New Year's celebration, renovations began to turn the dome into a sports complex, and it will be used for the 2012 Olympics.

WORLD'S LARGEST DOMES

Dome diameter, in feet (meters)

1,050 (320)	840 (256)	710 (216)	680 (210)	536 (163)
02, England	Georgia Dome, Georgia, USA	Reliant Astrodome, Texas, USA	Superdome, Louisiana, USA	Superior Dome, Michigan, USA

World's

TALLEST HABITABLE BUILDING

Taipei 101

Located in Taipei's Xinyi district, TAIPEI 101 towers over the city at a height of 1,666 feet (508 m). To reflect Taiwan's culture, the pagoda-style office building was designed to resemble sturdy bamboo stalks growing out of the ground. The 101-story building has 2.14 million square feet (198,348 sq m) of office space, and an additional 804,182 square feet (74,711 sq m) for a shopping center. As a safety precaution, the steel-frame building was built to withstand the country's strongest earthquakes and winds at a force of 134 miles (216 km) per hour.

83

WORLD'S TALLEST HABITABLE BUILDINGS

Height, in feet (meters)

1,666 (508)	1,483 (452)	1,454 (443)	1,381 (421)	1,362 (415)
Taipei 101, Taiwan	Petronas Twin Towers, Malaysia	Sears Tower, Chicago, USA	Jin Mao Building, China	Two International Finance Centre, China

84

World's

HIGHEST SUSPENSION BRIDGE

Royal Gorge

Located in Canon City, Colorado, the ROYAL GORGE BRIDGE spans the Arkansas River 1,053 feet (321 m) above the water. The bridge is 1,260 feet (384 m) long and 18 feet (5 m) wide. About 1,000 tons (907 t) of steel make up the bridge's floor, which can hold in excess of 2 million pounds (907,200 kg). The cables weigh about 300 tons (272 t) each. The bridge took just five months to complete in 1929, at a cost of $350,000.

WORLD'S HIGHEST SUSPENSION BRIDGES

Height, in feet (meters)

Royal Gorge, Colorado, USA	Viaduc de Millau, France	Tacoma Narrows, Washington, USA	Akashi-Kaikyo, Japan	Verrazano-Narrows, New York, USA
1,053 (321)	885 (270)	507 (155)	318 (97)	228 (69)

World's LONGEST SUSPENSION BRIDGE

CONSTRUCTIONS

Length of main span, in feet (meters)

6,529 (1,990)	5,320 (1,624)	4,888 (1,489)	4,626 (1,410)	4,544 (1,385)
Akashi-Kaikyo, Japan	Storebaelt, Denmark	Runyang, China	Humber Estuary, UK	Jiangyin, China

Akashi-Kaikyo

The **AKASHI-KAIKYO** connects Maiko, Tarumi Ward, in Kobe City, to Matsuho, Awaji Town, in Japan. Altogether, the suspension bridge spans the Akashi Strait for 2 miles (3 km) in Tsuna County on the Japanese island of Awajishima. Built in 1998, the structure's main span is a record-breaking 6,529 feet (1,990 m) long with cables supporting the 100,000-ton (90,700-t) bridge below. Each cable is made up of 290 strands of wire. The main tower soars approximately 984 feet (300 m) into the air. The bridge needed to be high above the water so it wouldn't block ships entering the Akashi Strait.

85

86

World's
MOST-VISITED CITY

New York City

In just one year, more than 46 million tourists visit NEW YORK CITY. That's the equivalent of the entire population of Canada coming for vacation! Both domestic and international travelers come to New York City to enjoy the theater and performing arts, museums, shopping, and historical landmarks. Collectively, visitors contribute more than $28 billion to the city's economy annually. Just more than 7 million tourists are from other countries, and most come from the United Kingdom, Canada, and Germany. During their stay, most travelers take advantage of the city's 72,250 hotel rooms and 18,800 restaurants.

WORLD'S MOST-VISITED CITIES

Annual visitors, in millions

New York City, USA	Tijuana, Mexico	San Diego, USA	London, England	Paris, France
46.0	39.6	31.1	27.3	27.0

World's
TOP TOURIST COUNTRY

France

FRANCE hosts more than 79 million tourists annually. That's more than twice the number of people living in all of the Northeast combined. The most popular French destinations are Paris and the Mediterranean coast. In July and August—the most popular months to visit France—tourists flock to the westernmost coastal areas of the region. In the winter, visitors hit the slopes at major ski resorts in the northern Alps. Tourists also visit many of France's world-renowned landmarks and monuments, including the Eiffel Tower, Notre Dame, the Louvre, and the Arc de Triomphe. Most tourists are from other European countries, especially Germany.

87

WORLD'S TOP TOURIST COUNTRIES

International visitors, in millions

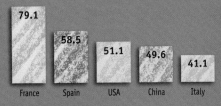

France	Spain	USA	China	Italy
79.1	58.5	51.1	49.6	41.1

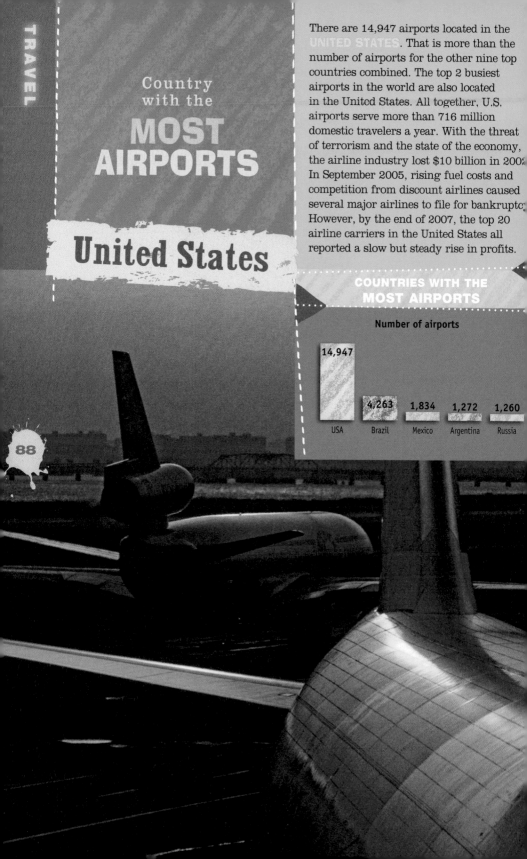

Country
with the
MOST
AIRPORTS

United States

There are 14,947 airports located in the UNITED STATES. That is more than the number of airports for the other nine top countries combined. The top 2 busiest airports in the world are also located in the United States. All together, U.S. airports serve more than 716 million domestic travelers a year. With the threat of terrorism and the state of the economy, the airline industry lost $10 billion in 2002. In September 2005, rising fuel costs and competition from discount airlines caused several major airlines to file for bankruptcy. However, by the end of 2007, the top 20 airline carriers in the United States all reported a slow but steady rise in profits.

COUNTRIES WITH THE MOST AIRPORTS

Number of airports

USA	Brazil	Mexico	Argentina	Russia
14,947	4,263	1,834	1,272	1,260

World's
BUSIEST AIRPORT

Hartsfield-Jackson Atlanta International Airport

The **HARTSFIELD-JACKSON ATLANTA INTERNATIONAL AIRPORT** serves almost 85 million travelers in one year. That's more people than are living in California, Texas, and Florida combined. Approximately 976,000 planes depart and arrive at this airport every year. With parking lots, runways, maintenance facilities, and other buildings, the Hartsfield terminal complex covers about 130 acres (53 ha). Hartsfield-Jackson Atlanta International Airport has a north and a south terminal, as well as an underground train, and six concourses that feature many shops, restaurants, and banks.

WORLD'S BUSIEST AIRPORTS

Annual passengers, in millions

84.8	77.0	67.5	65.8	61.0
Hartsfield-Jackson Atlanta Intl., USA	Chicago O'Hare Intl., USA	Heathrow Intl., England	Haneda Intl., Japan	Los Angeles Intl., USA

United States'
MOST-VISITED NATIONAL SITE

Blue Ridge Parkway

Each year more than 18 million people travel to North Carolina and Virginia to visit the BLUE RIDGE PARKWAY. The Blue Ridge is part of the eastern Appalachian Mountains and has an average elevation of 3,000 feet (914 m). The 469-mile (755-km) stretch of road winds through four national forests. Construction began on the country's first scenic parkway in 1935, and was completed in 1987. Some of the most popular activities along the Blue Ridge Parkway include hiking, camping, bicycling, and photographing nature.

90

UNITED STATES' MOST-VISITED NATIONAL SITES

Annual visitors, in millions

18.95	13.48	9.29	8.46	7.78
Blue Ridge Parkway, North Carolina–Virginia	Golden Gate National Recreation Area, California	Great Smoky Mountains, Tennessee–North Carolina	Gateway National Recreation Area, New Jersey–New York	Lake Mead National Recreation Area, Arizona–Nevada

Nature Records

Animals • Natural Formations

Food • Weather • Plants

Disasters

World's LARGEST CRUSTACEAN

Giant Spider Crab

The **GIANT SPIDER CRAB** has a 12-foot (3.7-m) wide leg span. That's almost wide enough to take up two parking spaces! The crab's body measures about 15 inches (38.1 cm) wide. Its ten long legs are jointed, and the first set has large claws at the end. The giant sea creature can weigh between 35 and 44 pounds (16 and 20 kg). It feeds on dead animals and shellfish it finds on the ocean floor. Giant spider crabs live in the deep water of the Pacific Ocean off southern Japan.

WORLD'S LARGEST CRUSTACEANS

Leg span, in feet (meters)

Giant Spider Crab	Alaskan King Crab	Kamchatka Crab	Red King Crab	Coconut Crab
12 (3.7)	5 (1.5)	4.9 (2.5)	3.6 (1.1)	2.5 (0.8)

World's
LOUDEST ANIMAL

Blue Whale

The loudest animal on Earth is the BLUE WHALE. The giant mammal's call can reach up to 188 decibels—about 40 decibels louder than a jet engine. The rumbling, low-frequency sounds of the blue whale can travel several miles underwater. The whale's whistling call can be heard for several hundred miles below the sea. Much of this whale chatter is used for communication, especially during the mating season. People cannot detect the whales' calls, however, because they are too low-pitched for humans' ears.

WORLD'S LOUDEST ANIMALS

Loudness, in decibels

Blue Whale	Sperm Whale	Dolphin	Fin Whale	Manatee
188	170	165	160	100

94

World's
BIGGEST FISH

Whale Shark

Although the average length of a WHALE SHARK is 30 feet (9 m), many have been known to reach up to 60 feet (18 m) long. That's the same length as two school buses! Whale sharks also weigh an average of 50,000 pounds (22,680 kg). As with most sharks, the females are larger than the males. Their mouths measure about 5 feet (1.5 m) long and contain about 3,000 teeth. Amazingly, these gigantic fish eat only microscopic plankton and tiny fish. They float near the surface looking for food.

WORLD'S BIGGEST FISH

Average weight, in pounds (kilograms)

Whale Shark	Basking Shark	Great White Shark	Greenland Shark	Tiger Shark
50,000 (22,680)	32,000 (14,515)	7,000 (3,175)	2,250 (1,020)	2,070 (939)

WORLD'S LARGEST PINNIPEDS

Length, in feet (meters)

Southern Elephant Seal	Northern Elephant Seal	Steller Sea Lion	Pacific Walrus	Atlantic Walrus
21.0 (6.4)	15.0 (4.6)	11.0 (3.4)	10.5 (3.2)	10.0 (3.0)

World's LARGEST PINNIPED

Southern Elephant Seal

The SOUTHERN ELEPHANT SEAL is the largest member of the seal and sea lion family (or pinnipeds), with bulls (males) measuring more than 21 feet (6.4 m) long and weighing up to 8,800 pounds (3,992 kg). This giant pinniped got its name from its wrinkled nose that resembles an elephant's trunk. Southern elephant seals are also amazing divers and can reach depths of 3,280 feet (1,000 m) for up to 2 hours. These smart animals are very social and live in large groups. Their largest colonies are found around South Georgia and Macquarie Island.

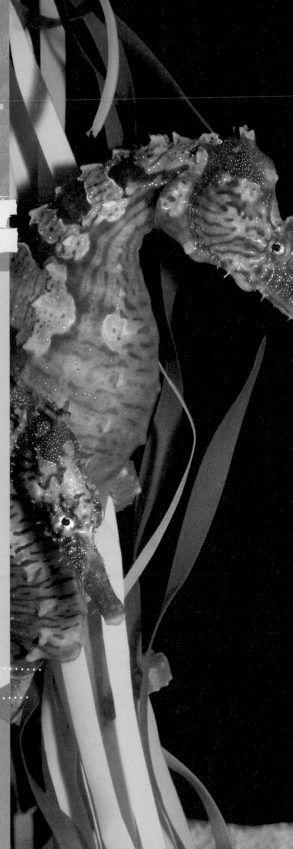

World's
SLOWEST FISH

Sea Horse

With a speed of just .001 miles (.002 km) per hour, SEA HORSES don't get anywhere fast. At that rate of speed, it would take the fish about an hour to swim only 5 feet (1.5 m). They range in size from less than half an inch (1 cm) to almost 1 foot (0.3 m). Sea horses spend most of their time near the shore. There, they can hold on to plants with their tails. This helps them avoid enemies. Approximately 50 different species of sea horses are found throughout the world. However, due to overharvesting, the sea horse population has decreased by up to 95%.

SOME OF THE WORLD'S SLOWEST FISH

Average speed, in miles (kilometers) per hour

Sea Horse	Barracuda	Tiger Shark	Tarpon	Swordfish
.001 (.002)	25 (40)	33 (53)	35 (56)	40 (64)

97

World's
FASTEST FISH

Sailfish

A SAILFISH once grabbed a fishing line and dragged it 300 feet (91 m) away in just 3 seconds. That means it was swimming at an average speed of 69 miles (109 km) per hour—just higher than the average speed limit on the highway! Sailfish are very large—they average 6 feet (1.8 m) long, but can grow up to 11 feet (3.4 m). Sailfish eat squid and surface-dwelling fish. Sometimes several sailfish will work together to catch their prey. They are found in both the Atlantic and Pacific oceans and prefer a water temperature of about 80°F (27°C).

WORLD'S FASTEST FISH

Maximum recorded speed, in miles (kilometers) per hour

Sailfish	Marlin	Bluefin Tuna	Yellowfin Tuna	Blue Shark
69 (109)	50 (80)	46 (74)	44 (70)	43 (69)

98

World's
LARGEST BIRD WINGSPAN

Marabou Stork

With a wingspan that can reach up to 13 feet (4 m), the MARABOU STORK has the largest wingspan of any bird. These large storks weigh up to 20 pounds (9 kg) and can grow up to 5 feet (150 cm) tall. Their long leg and toe bones are actually hollow. This adaptation is very important for flight because it makes the bird lighter. Although marabous eat insects, small mammals, and fish, the majority of their food is carrion—already-dead meat. In fact, the stork's head and neck do not have any feathers. This helps the bird stay clean as it sticks its head into carcasses to pick out scraps of food.

WORLD'S LARGEST BIRD WINGSPANS

Wingspan, in feet (meters)

Marabou Stork	Albatross	Trumpeter Swan	Mute Swan	Whooper Swan
13 (4)	12 (3.7)	11 (3.4)	10 (3)	10 (3)

World's
FASTEST FLIER

Peregrine Falcon

A PEREGRINE FALCON can reach speeds of up to 175 miles (282 km) per hour while diving through the air. That's about the same speed as the fastest race car in the Indianapolis 500. These powerful birds can catch prey in midair and kill it instantly with their sharp claws. Peregrine falcons range from about 13 to 19 inches (33 to 48 cm) long. The female is called a falcon, but the male is called a tercel, which means "one-third" in German. This is because the male is about one-third the size of the female.

99

WORLD'S
FASTEST FLIERS

Top speed, in miles (kilometers) per hour

175 (282)	106 (171)	95 (153)	88 (142)	80 (129)
Peregrine Falcon	Spine-tailed Swift	Frigate Bird	Spur-winged Goose	Red-breasted Merganser

World's
LONGEST BIRD MIGRATION

Arctic Tern

100

The ARCTIC TERN migrates from Maine to the coast of Africa, and then on to Antarctica, flying some 22,000 miles (35,406 km) a year. That's almost the same measurement as the Earth's circumference. Some don't complete the journey, however—young terns fly the first half of the journey with parents, but remain in Antarctica for a year or two. When they have matured, the birds fly back to Maine and the surrounding areas. Scientists are puzzled by how these birds remember the way back after only making the journey once so early in their lives.

WORLD'S
LONGEST BIRD MIGRATIONS

Round-trip migration, in miles (kilometers)

Arctic Tern	White-rumped Sandpiper	Red Knot	Lesser Yellowleg	Swainson's Hawk
22,000 (35,406)	20,000 (32,187)	20,000 (32,187)	18,000 (28,968)	15,000 (24,140)

Bird that Builds the
LARGEST NEST

Bald Eagle

With a nest that can measure 8 feet (2.4 m) wide and 16 feet (4.9 m) deep, BALD EAGLES have plenty of room to move around. These birds of prey have wingspans of up to 7.5 feet (2.3 m) and need a home that they can nest in comfortably. By carefully constructing their nest with sticks, branches, and plant material, a pair of bald eagles can balance their home—which can weigh up to 4,000 pounds (1,814 kg)—on the top of a tree or cliff. These nests are usually located by rivers or coastlines, the birds' watery hunting grounds. Called an aerie, this home will be used for the rest of the eagles' lives.

WORLD'S LARGEST BIRDS' NESTS

Diameter, in feet (meters)

Bald Eagles	Sociable Weavers	Maguari Storks	Great Blue Herons	Monk Parakeets
8 (2.4)	7 (2.1)	6 (1.8)	4.5 (1.4)	3 (0.9)

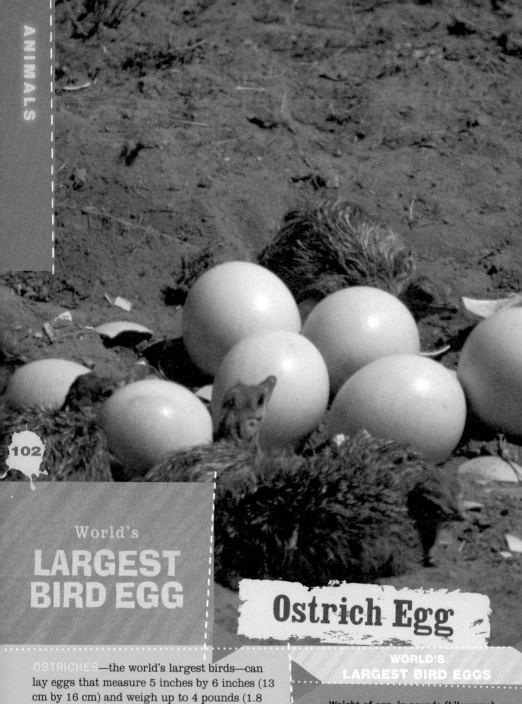

102

World's
LARGEST BIRD EGG

Ostrich Egg

OSTRICHES—the world's largest birds—can lay eggs that measure 5 inches by 6 inches (13 cm by 16 cm) and weigh up to 4 pounds (1.8 kg). In fact, just one ostrich egg equals up to 24 chicken eggs. The egg yolk makes up one-third of the volume. Although the eggshell is only .08 inch (2 mm) thick, it is tough enough to withstand the weight of a 345-pound (157-kg) ostrich. A hen ostrich can lay from 10 to 70 eggs each year. Females are usually able to recognize their own eggs, even when they are mixed in with those of other females in their shared nest.

WORLD'S LARGEST BIRD EGGS

Weight of egg, in pounds (kilograms)

Ostrich	Emu	Kiwi	Emperor Penguin	Albatross
4.0 (1.8)	1.8 (0.82)	1.6 (0.72)	1.5 (0.68)	1.0 (0.45)

FASTEST LAND BIRD

Ostrich

An OSTRICH can run at a top speed of 45 miles (72.4 km) per hour for about 30 minutes. This allows the speedy bird to easily outrun most predators. Its long, powerful legs help an ostrich cover 10 to 15 feet (3.1 to 4.6 km) per bound. And although it is a flightless bird, an ostrich uses it wings for balance when it runs. If an ostrich does need to defend itself, it has a kick powerful enough to kill a lion. The ostrich, which is also the world's largest bird at 10 feet (3.1 m) tall and 350 pounds (158.8 kg), is native to the savannas of Africa.

103

WORLD'S FASTEST LAND BIRDS

Speed, in miles (kilometers) per hour

45 (72.4)	40 (64.4)	30 (48.2)	20 (32.2)	17 (27.4)
Ostrich	Emu	Cassowary	Wild Turkey	Roadrunner

World's
FASTEST SHARK

Mako Shark

A MAKO SHARK can cruise through the water at 50 miles (79.4 km) per hour—about the speed limit of most highways. This super speed helps the shark catch its food, which consists mostly of tuna, herring, mackerel, swordfish, and porpoise. Occasionally makos even build up enough speed to leap out of the water. Mako sharks average 7 feet (2.1 m) in length, but can grow up to 12 feet (3.7 m) and weigh 1,000 pounds (454 kg). The sharks are found in temperate and tropical seas throughout the world.

WORLD'S FASTEST SHARKS

Fastest speed, in miles (kilometers) per hour

Mako Shark	Blue Shark	Great White Shark	Tiger Shark	Lemon Shark
50 (79.4)	43 (69.2)	25 (40.2)	22 (35.4)	20 (32.2)

105

World's HEAVIEST MARINE MAMMAL

Blue Whale

BLUE WHALES are the largest animals that have ever inhabited earth. They can weigh more than 143.3 tons (130 t) and measure over 100 feet (30 m) long. Amazingly, these gentle giants only eat krill—small, shrimplike animals. A blue whale can eat about 4 tons (3.6 t) of krill each day in the summer, when food is plentiful. To catch the krill, a whale gulps as much as 17,000 gallons (64,600 L) of seawater into its mouth at one time. Then it uses its tongue—which can be the same size as a car—to push the water back out. The krill get caught in hairs on the whale's baleen (a keratin structure that hangs down from the roof of the whale's mouth).

WORLD'S HEAVIEST MARINE MAMMALS

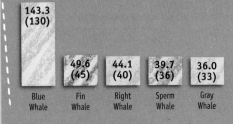

Weight, in tons (metric tons)

Blue Whale	Fin Whale	Right Whale	Sperm Whale	Gray Whale
143.3 (130)	49.6 (45)	44.1 (40)	39.7 (36)	36.0 (33)

106

World's
HEAVIEST LAND MAMMAL

African Elephant

Weighing in at up to 14,430 pounds (6,545 kg) and measuring approximately 24 feet (7.3 m) long, AFRICAN ELEPHANTS are truly humongous. Even at their great size, they are strictly vegetarian. They will, however, eat up to 500 pounds (226 kg) of vegetation a day! Their two tusks—which are really elongated teeth—grow continuously during their lives and can reach about 9 feet (2.7 m) in length. Elephants live in small groups of 8 to 15 family members with one female (called a cow) as the leader.

WORLD'S HEAVIEST LAND MAMMALS

Weight, in pounds (kilograms)

African Elephant	White Rhinoceros	Hippopotamus	Giraffe	American Bison
14,430 (6,545)	7,937 (3,600)	5,512 (2,300)	3,527 (1,600)	2,205 (1,000)

World's
LARGEST RODENT

Capybara

CAPYBARAS reach an average length of 4 feet (1.2 m), stand about 20 inches (51 cm) tall, and weigh between 75 and 150 pounds (34 to 68 kg)! That's about the same size as a Labrador retriever. Also known as water hogs and carpinchos, capybaras are found in South and Central America, where they spend much of their time in groups looking for food. They are strictly vegetarian and have been known to raid gardens for melons and squash. Their partially webbed feet make capybaras excellent swimmers. They can dive down to the bottom of a lake or river to find plants and stay there for up to five minutes.

107

WORLD'S LARGEST RODENTS

Maximum weight, in pounds (kilograms)

150 (68)
Capybara

57 (26)
Porcupine

33 (15)
Pacarana

33 (15)
Patagonian Cavy

20 (8)
Plains Viscacha

World's
SLOWEST LAND MAMMAL

Three-toed Sloth

108

A THREE-TOED SLOTH can reach a top speed of only .07 miles (.11 km) per hour while traveling on the ground. That means that it would take the animal almost 15 minutes to cross a four-lane street. The main reason sloths move so slowly is that they cannot walk like other mammals. They must pull themselves along the ground using only their sharp claws. Because of this, sloths spend the majority of their time in trees. There, they will sleep up to 18 hours each day. When they wake at night, they search for leaves and shoots to eat.

SOME OF THE WORLD'S SLOWEST LAND MAMMALS

Maximum speed, in miles (kilometers) per hour

Three-toed Sloth	Koala	Gibbon	Pig	Squirrel
.07 (.11)	7 (11.3)	10 (16.1)	11 (18)	12 (19)

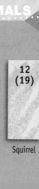

109

World's
FASTEST LAND MAMMAL

Cheetah

For short spurts these sleek mammals can reach a speed of 65 miles (105 km) per hour. They can accelerate from 0 to 40 miles (64 km) per hour in just three strides. Their quickness easily enables these large African cats to outrun their prey. All other African cats must stalk their prey because they lack the CHEETAH's amazing speed. Unlike the paws of all other cats, cheetah paws do not have skin sheaths (thin protective coverings). Their claws, therefore, cannot pull back.

WORLD'S FASTEST LAND MAMMALS

Maximum speed, in miles (kilometers) per hour

Cheetah	Pronghorn Antelope	Mongolian Gazelle	Springbok	Grant's Gazelle/ Thompson's Gazelle
65 (105)	55 (89)	50 (80)	50 (80)	47 (76)

110

World's
TALLEST LAND ANIMAL

Giraffe

GIRAFFES are the giants among mammals, growing to more than 18 feet (5.5 m) in height. That means an average giraffe could look through the window of a two-story building. A giraffe's neck is 18 times longer than a human's, but both mammals have exactly the same number of neck bones. A giraffe's long legs enable it to outrun most of its enemies. When cornered, a giraffe has been known to kill a lion with a single kick.

SOME OF THE WORLD'S TALLEST ANIMALS

Height, in feet (meters)

18 (5.5)	7 (2.1)	6.5 (2)	6 (1.8)	5 (1.5)
Giraffe	African Elephant	Camel	Moose	Rhino

World's LARGEST BAT

Giant Flying Fox

A GIANT FLYING FOX—a member of the megabat family—can have a wingspan of up to 6 feet (2 m). These furry mammals average just 7 wing beats per second, but can travel more than 40 miles (64 km) a night in search of food. Unlike smaller bats, flying foxes rely on their acute vision and sense of smell to locate fruit, pollen, and nectar. Flying foxes got their name because their faces resemble a fox's face. Megabats live in the tropical areas of Africa, Asia, and Australia.

111

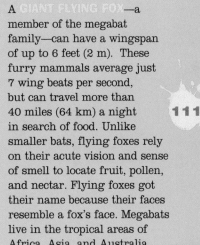

WORLD'S LARGEST BATS

Wingspan, in feet (meters)

6.0 (1.8)	5.7 (1.7)	5.5 (1.7)	5.0 (1.5)	4.4 (1.3)
Giant Flying Fox	Malayan Flying Fox	Golden Crown	Lyle's Flying Fox	Indian Flying Fox

World's
MOST DEADLY AMPHIBIAN

Poison Dart Frog

POISON DART FROGS are found mostly in the tropical rain forests of Central and South America, where they live on the moist land. These lethal amphibians have enough poison to kill up to 20 humans. A dart frog's poison is so effective that native Central and South Americans sometimes coat their hunting arrows or hunting darts with it. These brightly colored frogs can be yellow, orange, red, green, blue, or any combination of these colors and measure only 0.5 to 2 inches (1 to 5 cm) long. There are approximately 75 different species of poison dart frogs.

SOME OF THE WORLD'S MOST POISONOUS AMPHIBIANS

Risk of fatality

Extreme	High	Medium	Medium	Medium
Poison Dart Frog	Black and Yellow Spotted Frog	Fire-bellied Toad	European Salamander	Cane Toad

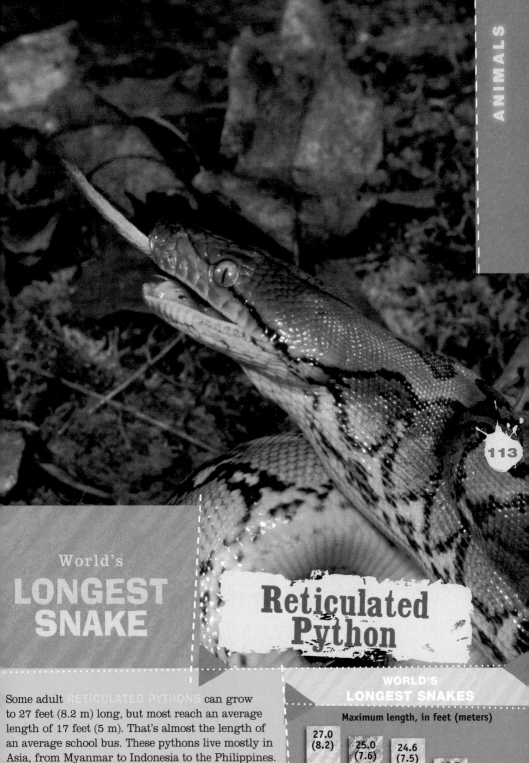

113

World's
LONGEST SNAKE

Reticulated Python

Some adult RETICULATED PYTHONS can grow to 27 feet (8.2 m) long, but most reach an average length of 17 feet (5 m). That's almost the length of an average school bus. These pythons live mostly in Asia, from Myanmar to Indonesia to the Philippines. The python has teeth that curve backward and can hold the snake's prey still. It hunts mainly at night and will eat mammals and birds. Reticulated pythons are slow-moving creatures that kill their prey by constriction, or strangulation.

WORLD'S LONGEST SNAKES

Maximum length, in feet (meters)

Reticulated Python	Anaconda	Rock Python	King Cobra	Oriental Rat Snake
27.0 (8.2)	25.0 (7.6)	24.6 (7.5)	17.7 (5.4)	12.2 (3.7)

114

Snake with the
LONGEST FANGS

Gaboon Viper

The fangs of a GABOON VIPER measure 2 inches (5 cm) in length! These giant fangs fold up against the snake's mouth so it does not pierce its own skin. When it is ready to strike its prey, the fangs snap down into position. The snake can grow up to 7 feet (2 m) long and weigh 18 pounds (8 kg). It is found in Africa and is perfectly camouflaged for hunting on the ground beneath leaves and grasses. The Gaboon viper's poison is not as toxic as some other snakes', but it is quite dangerous because of the amount of poison it can inject at one time. The snake is not very aggressive, however, and usually only attacks when bothered.

SNAKES WITH THE LONGEST FANGS

Fang length, in inches (centimeters)

2.0 (5.1) — Gaboon Viper

1.5 (3.8) — Bushmaster

1.0 (2.5) — Black Mamba

1.0 (2.5) — Diamondback Rattlesnake

0.7 (1.8) — Australian Taipan

ANIMALS

World's
DEADLIEST SNAKE

Black Mamba

Deaths possible per bite

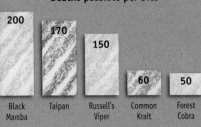

Black Mamba	Taipan	Russell's Viper	Common Krait	Forest Cobra
200	170	150	60	50

With just one bite, an African BLACK MAMBA snake releases a venom powerful enough to kill up to 200 humans. A bite from this snake is almost always fatal if it is not treated immediately. This large member of the cobra family grows to about 14 feet (4.3 m) long. In addition to its deadly poison, it is also a very aggressive snake. It will raise its body off the ground when it feels threatened. It then spreads its hood and strikes swiftly at its prey with its long front teeth. A black mamba is also very fast—it can move along at about 7 miles (11.7 km) per hour for short bursts.

115

World's
LARGEST AMPHIBIAN

Chinese Giant Salamander

With a length of 6 feet (1.8 m) and a weight of 55 pounds (25 kg), CHINESE GIANT SALAMANDERS rule the amphibi world. This amphibian has a large head, but its eyes and nostrils are small. It has short legs, a long tail, and very smooth skin. This large amphibian can be found in the streams of northeastern, central, and southern China. It feeds on fish, frogs, crabs, and snakes. The Chinese giant salamander will not hunt its prey. It will wait until a potential meal wanders too close and then grab it in its mouth. Because many people enjoy the taste of th salamander's meat, it is often hunted and its population is shrinking.

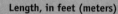

WORLD'S LARGEST AMPHIBIANS

Length, in feet (meters)

6 (1.8)	5.7 (1.7)	4.8 (1.5)	2.4 (0.7)	1.4 (0.4)
Chinese Giant Salamander	Giant Japanese Salamander	Caecilia Thompsoni	Hellbender	Goliath Frog

Komodo Dragon

117

LONGEST-LIVED REPTILE

Galápagos Tortoise

Some GALÁPAGOS TORTOISES have been known to live to the old age of 150 years. Galápagos tortoises are also some of the largest tortoises in the world, weighing in at up to 500 pounds (226 kg). Even at their great size, these creatures can pull their heads, tails, and legs completely inside their shells. Amazingly, Galápagos tortoises can go without eating or drinking for many weeks. Approximately 10,000 of these tortoises live on the Galápagos island chain west of Ecuador.

WORLD'S LONGEST-LIVED REPTILES

Maximum age, in years

Galápagos Tortoise	Box Turtle	American Alligator	Boa Constrictor	Komodo Dragon
150	120	50	30	20

118

World's
LARGEST LIZARD

Komodo Dragon

With a length of 10 feet (3 m) and a weight of 300 pounds (136 kg), KOMODO DRAGONS are the largest lizards roaming the Earth. A Komodo dragon has a long neck and tail, and strong legs. These members of the monitor family are found mainly on Komodo Island, located in the Lesser Sunda Islands of Indonesia. Komodos are dangerous and have even been known to attack and kill humans. A Komodo uses its sense of smell to locate food. It uses its long, yellow tongue to pick up an animal's scent. A Komodo can consume 80% of its body weight in just one meal!

WORLD'S LARGEST LIZARDS

Length, in feet (meters)

10.0 (3.0)	8.8 (2.7)	7.8 (2.4)	5.0 (1.5)	5.0 (1.5)
Komodo Dragon	Water Monitor	Perenty	Common Iguana	Marine Iguana

World's
LARGEST REPTILE

Saltwater Crocodile

SALTWATER CROCODILES can grow to more than 22 feet (6.7 m) long. That's about twice the length of the average car. However, males usually measure only about 17 feet (5 m) long, and females normally reach about 10 feet (3 m) in length. A large adult will feed on buffalo, monkeys, cattle, wild boar, and other large mammals. Saltwater crocodiles are found throughout the East Indies and Australia. Despite their name, saltwater crocodiles can also be found in fresh water and swamps. Some other common names for this species are the estuary crocodile and the Indo-Pacific crocodile.

119

WORLD'S LARGEST REPTILES

Maximum length, in feet (meters)

22 (6.7)	21 (6.4)	20 (6.2)	20 (6.2)	13 (3.9)
Saltwater Crocodile	Gharial	Black Caiman	Orinoco Crocodile	American Alligator

World's
LARGEST SPIDER

Goliath Birdeater

A GOLIATH BIRDEATER is about the same size as a dinner plate—it can grow to a total length of 11 inches (28 cm) and weigh about 6 ounces (170 g). A Goliath's spiderlings are also big—they can have a 6-inch (15-cm) leg span after just one year. These giant tarantulas are found mostly in the rain forests of Guyana, Suriname, Brazil, and Venezuela. The Goliath birdeater's name is misleading—they commonly eat insects and small reptiles. Similar to other tarantula species, the Goliath birdeater lives in a burrow. The spider will wait by the opening to ambush prey that gets too close.

WORLD'S LARGEST SPIDERS

Length, in inches (centimeters)

Goliath Birdeater	Salmon Pink Birdeater	Slate Red Ornamental	King Baboon	Colombian Giant Redleg
11 (28)	10.5 (27)	9 (23)	8 (20)	8 (20)

World's
FASTEST-FLYING INSECT

Hawk Moth

The average HAWK MOTH—which got its name from its swift and steady flight—can cruise along at speeds over 33 miles (53 km) per hour. That's faster than the average speed limit on most city streets. Although they are found throughout the world, most species live in tropical climates. Also known as the sphinx moth and the hummingbird moth, this large insect can have a wingspan that reaches up to 8 inches (20 cm). The insect also has a good memory and may return to the same flowers at the same time each day.

WORLD'S FASTEST-FLYING INSECTS

Speed, in miles (kilometers) per hour

Hawk Moth	West Indian Butterfly	Deer Botfly	Dragonfly	Hornet
33.3 (53.6)	30.0 (48.2)	30.0 (48.2)	17.9 (28.6)	13.3 (21.4)

122

World's
FASTEST-RUNNING INSECT

Australian Tiger Beetle

AUSTRALIAN TIGER BEETLES can zip along at about 5.7 miles (9.2 km) per hour—that's about 170 body lengths per second! If a human could run at the same pace, he or she would run about 340 miles (547.2 km) per hour. Australian tiger beetles use their terrific speed to run down prey. Once a meal has been caught, the beetle chews it up in its powerful jaws and coats it in digestive juice. When the prey has become soft, the tiger beetle rolls it together and eats. These fierce beetles, which got their name from their skillful hunting, will also bite humans when provoked.

WORLD'S FASTEST-RUNING INSECTS

Speed, in miles (kilometers) per hour

5.7 (9.2)	3.5 (5.6)	1.2 (1.9)	1.0 (1.6)	0.8 (1.3)
Australian Tiger Beetle	American Cockroach	Centipede	Ant	Mother-of-Pearl Caterpillar

World's
LONGEST INSECT MIGRATION

Monarch Butterfly

Millions of MONARCH BUTTERFLIES travel to Mexico from all parts of North America every fall, flying up to 2,700 miles (4,345 km). Once there, they will huddle together in the trees and wait out the cold weather. In spring and summer, most butterflies only live four or five weeks as adults, but in the fall, a special generation of monarchs is born. These butterflies will live for about seven months and participate in the great migration to Mexico. Scientists are studying these butterflies in hope of learning how the insects know where and when to migrate to a place they— or several generations before them—have never visited.

123

WORLD'S LONGEST INSECT MIGRATIONS

Migration, in miles (kilometers)

Monarch Butterfly	Desert Locust	Painted Lady Butterfly	Diamondback Moth	Ladybug
2,700 (4,345)	2,600 (4,184)	2,500 (4,023)	1,850 (2,977)	300 (483)

124

World's
TALLEST MOUNTAIN

Mount Everest

MOUNT EVEREST's tallest peak towers 29,035 feet (8,850 m) into the air, and it is the highest point on Earth. This peak is an unbelievable 5.5 miles (8.8 km) above sea level. Mount Everest is located in the Himalayas, on the border between Nepal and Tibet. The mountain got its official name from surveyor Sir George Everest. In 1953, Sir Edmund Hillary and Tenzing Norgay were the first people to reach the peak. In 2008, the Olympic torch was carried up to the top of the mountain on its way to the games in Beijing.

WORLD'S TALLEST MOUNTAINS

Highest point, in feet (meters)

29,035 (8,850)	28,250 (8,611)	28,169 (8,586)	27,940 (8,516)	27,766 (8,463)
Mount Everest, Asia	K2, Asia	Kangchenjunga, Asia	Lhotse, Asia	Makalu, Asia

WORLD'S TALLEST VOLCANOES

Height, in feet (meters)

22,595 (6,887)	22,057 (6,723)	21,850 (6,660)	21,430 (6,532)	20,922 (6,398)
Ojos del Salado, Argentina/ Chile	Llullaillaco, Argentina/ Chile	Tipas, Argentina	Cerro el Cóndor, Argentina	Coropuna, Peru

World's
TALLEST VOLCANO

Ojos del Salado

Located on the border of Argentina and Chile, OJOS DEL SALADO towers 22,595 feet (6,887 m) above the surrounding Atacama Desert. It is the second-highest peak in the Andean mountain chain. Ojos del Salado is a composite volcano, which means that it is a tall, symmetrical cone that was built by layers of lava flow, ash, and cinder. There is no record of the volcano erupting, but this could be because of the volcano's remote location. Ojos del Salado is a very popular spot for mountain climbing.

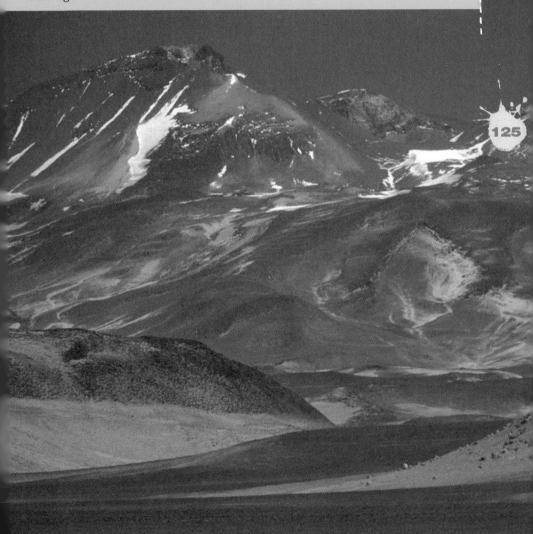

125

World's
LARGEST LAKE

Caspian Sea

This giant inland body of saltwater stretches for almost 750 miles (1,207 km) from north to south, with an average width of about 200 miles (322 km). All together, it covers an area that's almost the same size as the state of California. The CASPIAN SEA is located east of the Caucasus Mountains in Central Asia. It is bordered by Iran, Russia, Kazakhstan, Azerbaijan, and Turkmenistan. The Caspian Sea has an average depth of about 550 feet (170 m). It is an important fishing resource, with species including sturgeon, salmon, perch, herring, and carp. Other animals live in the Caspian Sea, including porpoises, seals, and tortoises. The sea is estimated to be 30 million years old and became landlocked 5.5 million years ago.

126

WORLD'S LARGEST LAKES

Approximate area, in square miles (square kilometers)

Caspian Sea, Asia	Superior, N. America	Victoria, Africa	Huron, N. America	Michigan, N. America
143,200 (370,901)	31,820 (82,413)	26,570 (68,816)	23,010 (59,596)	22,400 (58,016)

World's
LARGEST
DESERT

Sahara

Located in northern Africa, the SAHARA DESERT covers approximately 3.5 million square miles (9.1 million sq km). It stretches for 5,200 miles (8,372 km) through the countries of Morocco, Algeria, Tunisia, Libya, Egypt, Mauritania, Mali, Niger, Chad, and Sudan. The Sahara gets very little rainfall—less than 8 inches (20 cm) per year. Even with its harsh environment, some 2.5 million people—mostly nomads—call the Sahara home. Date palms and acacias grow near oases. Some of the animals that live in the Sahara include gazelles, antelopes, jackals, foxes, and badgers.

127

WORLD'S
LARGEST DESERTS

Area, in millions of
square miles (square kilometers)

3.5 (9.1)	1.4 (3.6)	0.5 (1.3)	0.4 (1.0)	0.2 (0.5)
Sahara, Africa	Australian, Australia	Arabian, Africa	Gobi, Asia	Kalahari, Africa

128

World's
LONGEST RIVER

Nile

The NILE RIVER in Africa stretches 4,145 miles (6,671 km), from the tributaries of Lake Victoria in Tanzania and Uganda out to the Mediterranean Sea. Because of varying depths, boats can sail on only about 2,000 miles (3,217 km) of the river. The Nile flows through Rwanda, Uganda, Sudan, and Egypt. The river's water supply is crucial to the existence of these African countries. The Nile's precious water is used to irrigate crops and to generate electricity. The Aswan Dam and the Aswan High Dam—both located in Egypt—are used to store the autumn floodwater for later use. The Nile is also used to transport goods from city to city along the river.

Total length, in miles (kilometers)

Nile, Africa	Amazon, S. America	Mississippi-Missouri, N. America	Yangtze-Kiang, Asia	Yenisei, Angara, Asia
4,145 (6,671)	4,000 (6,437)	3,740 (6,021)	3,720 (5,987)	3,650 (5,877)

World's
GREATEST-FLOWING RIVER

Amazon

The AMAZON RIVER moves more water than any other river in the world. It empties 58 billion gallons (220,000 cu m) per second into the Atlantic Ocean. At 4,000 miles (6,566 km), the Amazon is the second-longest river in the world. It contains more water than the Nile, Mississippi, and Yangtze rivers combined, and makes up more than 20% of the Earth's fresh water. The Amazon is also the world's widest river, measuring up to 7 miles (11 km) from bank to bank. The mouth of the Amazon measures about 200 miles (322 km), and contains the Marajó—the world's largest freshwater island.

129

WORLD'S GREATEST-FLOWING RIVERS

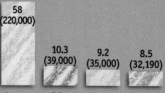

Average flow per second, in billions of gallons (cubic meters)

58 (220,000)	10.3 (39,000)	9.2 (35,000)	8.5 (32,190)	6.7 (25,200)
Amazon, S. America	Zaire, Africa	Negro, S. America	Yangtze-Kiang, Asia	Orinoco, S. America

World's
LARGEST OCEAN

Pacific

The PACIFIC OCEAN covers
almost 64 million square
miles (166 million sq km) and
reaches 36,200 feet (11,000 m)
below sea level at its greatest
depth—the Mariana Trench
(near the Philippines). In fact,
this ocean is so large that
it covers about one-third of
the planet (more than all of
Earth's land put together)
and holds more than half of
all the seawater on Earth. The
United States could fit inside
this ocean 18 times! Some
of the major bodies of water
included in the Pacific are the
Bering Sea, the Coral Sea, the
Philippine Sea, and the Gulf of
Alaska.

130

WORLD'S LARGEST OCEANS

Maximum area, in millions of
square miles (square kilometers)

64.0 (165.7)	31.8 (82.4)	25.3 (65.5)	5.4 (14.0)
Pacific Ocean	Atlantic Ocean	Indian Ocean	Arctic Ocean

131

World's
LONGEST MOUNTAIN CHAIN

Andes

For 5,000 miles (8,050 km) the ANDES extend through seven countries of South America—Venezuela, Colombia, Ecuador, Peru, Bolivia, Chile, and Argentina. The Andes also have some of the highest peaks in the world, with more than fifty of them measuring above 20,000 feet (6,100 m). Some of the animals found in the Andes include wild horses; vicuñas, members of the camel family; and chinchillas, furry members of the rodent family. The condor—the world's largest bird of prey—also calls these mountains its home.

WORLD'S LONGEST MOUNTAIN CHAINS

Length, in miles (kilometers)

5,000 (8,050)	2,200 (3,542)	2,000 (3,220)	1,900 (3,059)	1,600 (2,576)
Andes, S. America	Transantarctic Mountains, Antarctica	Rocky Mountains, USA	Great Dividing Range, Australia	Himalayas, Asia

132

World's
LARGEST ISLAND

Greenland

Located in the North Atlantic Ocean, GREENLAND covers more than 840,000 square miles (2,175,600 sq km). Not including continents, it is the largest island in the world. Its jagged coastline is approximately 24,400 miles (39,267 km) long—about the same distance as Earth's circumference at the equator. Mountain chains are located on Greenland's east and west coasts, and the coastline is indented by fjords, or thin bodies of water bordered by steep cliffs. From north to south, the island stretches for about 1,660 miles (2,670 km). About 700,000 square miles (1,813,000 sq km) of this massive island are covered by a giant ice sheet. The island also contains the world's largest national park—Northeast Greenland National Park—with an area of 375,291 square miles (972,000 sq km).

WORLD'S LARGEST ISLANDS

Approximate area, in square miles (square kilometers)

Greenland	New Guinea	Borneo	Madagascar	Baffin Island
840,070 (2,175,600)	312,190 (808,572)	289,961 (751,000)	226,674 (587,086)	195,926 (507,448)

Country with the

MOST TROPICAL RAIN FORESTS

Brazil

BRAZIL—a large, tropical country in South America—has almost 1.16 million square miles (3.0 million sq km) of rain forest. The tropical forests of the Amazon River are located in the northern and north-central areas of the country. Amazonia, the world's largest rain forest, spreads across half of Brazil. The rain forest is home to 2.5 million insects, 500 mammal species, 300 reptile species, and a third of the world's birds. The rain forest is threatened, however, by timber companies, the growing human population, and ranchers clearing land for their herds to graze.

133

COUNTRIES WITH THE MOST TROPICAL RAIN FORESTS

Area, in square miles (square kilometers)

Brazil, S. America	Democratic Republic of Congo, Africa	Indonesia, Asia	Peru, S. America	Bolivia, S. America
1,159,359 (3,002,726)	515,871 (1,336,100)	341,681 (884,950)	265,414 (687,419)	226,796 (587,398)

Country with the

LONGEST COASTLINE

Canada

CANADA's coastline measures 125,566 miles (202,079 km). If someone walked 12.5 miles (20.1 km) a day, it would take him or her about 33 years to walk its length. This measurement includes the mainland coast, as well as the coasts of the offshore islands. Of all the provinces and territories, Nunavut has the most coastline with 70,777 miles (113,904 km). The Canadian coast is made up of sandy beaches, towering cliffs, mudflats, marshes, and rocky piles. It also touches three oceans: the Pacific, the Atlantic, and the Arctic.

COUNTRIES WITH THE LONGEST COASTLINES

Total coastline, in miles (kilometers)

Canada	Indonesia	Russia	Philippines	Japan
125,566 (202,079)	33,999 (54,717)	23,396 (37,652)	22,559 (36,305)	18,486 (29,750)

134

135

World's
LARGEST DIAMOND

Golden Jubilee

The GOLDEN JUBILEE is the world's largest faceted diamond, with a weight of 545.67 carats. This gigantic gem got its name when it was presented to the king of Thailand in 1997 for the Golden Jubilee—or 50th anniversary celebration—of his reign. The diamond was discovered in a South African mine in 1986 weighing 755.5 carats. Once it was cut, the diamond featured 148 perfectly symmetrical facets. The process took almost a year because of the diamond's size and multiple tension points. The diamond is on display at the Royal Museum of Bangkok in Thailand.

WORLD'S LARGEST DIAMONDS

Weight, in carats

Golden Jubilee	Great Star of Africa	Incomparable/ Zale	Second Star of Africa	Centenary
545.67	530.20	317.40	317.40	273.85

136

World's
LARGEST FRUIT CROP

Tomatoes

More than 125 million tons (113.4 million t) of TOMATOES are produced throughout the world each year. The world's top producers include the United States, Spain, Italy, Turkey, and China. Within the United States, about 180 square miles (466.2 sq km) are dedicated to growing the juicy, red fruit. California alone produces almost 11 million tons (9.9 million t). There is occasionally some confusion about whether the tomato is a fruit or vegetable. This is usually because cooks use the tomato as a vegetable, but scientists classify it as a fruit.

WORLD'S LARGEST FRUIT CROPS

Production, in
millions of tons (metric tons)

Tomatoes	Watermelons	Bananas	Grapes	Apples
125.0 (113.4)	92.4 (83.8)	80.6 (73.1)	72.5 (65.8)	61.7 (56.0)

World's
LARGEST VEGETABLE CROP

Sugar Cane

More than 1.42 billion tons (1.29 billion t) of SUGAR CANE is produced worldwide each year. Sugar cane is a type of tropical grass that resembles bamboo. The stalk takes about a year to mature and can grow to 16.5 feet (5 m) high. The stalks are shredded and crushed to extract the juice, which is then heated and cooled to form sugar crystals. Sugar cane is used to produce about 70% of the world's sugar. About 105 countries grow the crop, and the top producers are Brazil and India.

137

WORLD'S LARGEST VEGETABLE CROPS

Production, in millions of tons (metric tons)

Sugar Cane	Potatoes	Sugar Beets	Soybeans	Sweet Potatoes
1,423 (1,290)	356 (323)	266 (241)	236 (214)	143 (130)

Country that Eats the
MOST VEGETABLES

Greece

The people of GREECE eat more than 600 pounds (272 kg) of vegetables per capita each year. Some of the most popular vegetables in Greek cuisine include eggplants, okra, zucchini, potatoes, and green beans. Approximately four-fifths of Greece is mountainous, which makes farming difficult. Only about 3% of the cultivated areas can be used for vegetable crops. Most of the country's vegetables are grown on the plains of Thessaly, Macedonia, and Thrace.

COUNTRIES THAT EAT THE MOST VEGETABLES

Annual per capita consumption, in pounds (kilograms)

Greece	United Arab Emirates	China	Lebanon	Libya
601 (273)	571 (259)	531 (241)	522 (237)	520 (236)

COUNTRIES THAT EAT THE MOST POTATO CHIPS

Annual per capita consumption, in pounds (kilograms)

UK	New Zealand	Australia	Ireland	USA
6.5 (2.9)	5.9 (2.7)	5.8 (2.6)	5.7 (2.6)	5.4 (2.5)

Country that Eats the
MOST POTATO CHIPS

United Kingdom

People in the UNITED KINGDOM eat a lot of chips—averaging about 6.5 pounds (2.9 kg) per capita each year. This means that each person snacks on almost 14 bags in just 12 months, and some 8.5 billion packages are sold each year! Better known as "crisps" in the United Kingdom, potato chips were first served in 1853 at a lodge in Saratoga Springs, New York. It takes about 10,000 pounds (4,536 kg) of potatoes to make 3,500 pounds (1,588 kg) of chips.

140

Country that Drinks the
MOST BOTTLED WATER

Italy

Italians like their bottled water—each person in the country drinks more than 46 gallons (174 L) of it each year. That averages to about a bottle and a half each day. The total amount of bottled water consumed in ITALY each year averages 2.8 billion gallons (10.6 billion L). There are about 175 mineral water sources in the country, which supply 280 brands of Italian bottled water. Some of the most popular brands include San Pellegrino, San Gimignano, Ferrarelle, Aqua Panna, Lurisia, and Fiuggi. There are 700 different brands of bottled water sold worldwide.

COUNTRIES THAT DRINK THE MOST BOTTLED WATER

Annual per capita consumption, in gallons (liters)

Italy	Spain	Mexico	France	Belgium
46.1 (174.5)	41.5 (157.1)	40.7 (154.1)	40.1 (151.8)	36.2 (137.0)

MOST SOFT DRINKS

United States

Americans have an annual per capita soft drink consumption of 53.8 gallons (203.7 L). This means that each person in the country drinks an average of 574 cans of soda each year. Soda accounts for about 25% of all drinks consumed in the UNITED STATES. About 77% of all soda is sold in containers, and the rest is sold through drink fountains. Recent studies show that diet sodas, as well as flavored sodas such as cherry, orange, and root beer, are becoming more popular than colas. The country's three top-selling soft drink companies are the Coca-Cola Company, PepsiCo Inc., and Dr Pepper/7UP.

141

COUNTRIES THAT CONSUME THE MOST SOFT DRINKS

Annual per capita consumption, in gallons (liters)

USA	Mexico	Norway	Ireland	Canada
53.8 (203.7)	33.3 (126.1)	31.9 (120.8)	31.6 (119.6)	30.7 (116.2)

Country that
Eats the

MOST CHOCOLATE

Switzerland

The per capita chocolate consumption in SWITZERLAND is 22.4 pounds (10.2 kg) per year. That means approximately 169 million pounds (77 million kg) of chocolate are eaten in this small country each year. The Swiss chocolate market totaled more than $894 million in 2005. Chocolate has always been a popular food around the world. In fact, each year, approximately 594,000 tons (538,758 t) of cocoa beans—an important ingredient in chocolate—are consumed worldwide. Chocolate is consumed mainly in the form of candy.

COUNTRIES THAT EAT THE MOST CHOCOLATE

Annual per capita consumption, in pounds (kilograms)

22.4 (10.2)	20.1 (9.1)	19.5 (8.9)	18.1 (8.2)	17.9 (8.1)
Switzerland	Austria	Ireland	Germany	Norway

Country that Eats the
MOST ICE CREAM

New Zealand

Each person in NEW ZEALAND eats an average of 56 pints (26.5 L) of ice cream every year. That's more than 1 pint per week. New Zealand also makes a lot of ice cream—about 15,000 tons (13,608 t) a year. The top flavors in New Zealand include vanilla, hokey pokey (vanilla with toffee bits), chocolate, and strawberry. Frozen treats were first served in the Roman Empire when people mixed fruit with ice. In the eighteenth century, ice cream became popular in France, England, and the United States. The ice-cream cone was first served in 1904 at the World's Fair in St. Louis, Missouri. Today, frozen dessert sales total billions of dollars worldwide.

COUNTRIES THAT EAT THE MOST ICE-CREAM

Annual per capita consumption, in pints (liters)

New Zealand	USA	Australia	Finland	Sweden
56.0 (26.5)	46.4 (22.0)	42.3 (20.0)	27.9 (13.2)	26.6 (12.6)

144

Country that Eats the
MOST MEAT

United States

Each person in the UNITED STATES will eat more than 269 pounds (122 kg) of meat this year. That's the same weight as 78 phone books. Beef is the most commonly eaten meat in the United States. Each American eats about 67 pounds (29.9 kg) of beef per year. In fact, an average 55 million pounds (24.9 million kg) of beef are eaten in the United States each day. The most common way to eat beef is in the form of a hamburger or cheeseburger. More than 85% of U.S. citizens ate one of these fast food items last year. Chicken is the second most popular meat, with each American eating about 87 pounds (39.5 kg) per year.

COUNTRIES THAT EAT THE MOST MEAT

Annual per capita consumption, in pounds (kilograms)

USA	Denmark	Spain	Australia	New Zealand
269.3 (122.2)	252.6 (114.6)	250.6 (113.7)	242.9 (110.2)	235.2 (106.7)

United States'
GREATEST SNOWFALL

Highest annual snowfall, in inches (centimeters)

Mount Rainier, Washington, 1971–1972	Mount Baker, Washington, 1998–1999	Paradise Station, Washington, 1971–1972	Thompson Pass, Alaska, 1952–1953
1,224 (3,109)	1,140 (2,895)	1,122 (2,849)	974 (2,474)

Mount Rainier

MOUNT RAINIER had a record snowfall of 1,224 inches (3,109 cm) between 1971 and 1972. That's enough snow to cover a 10-story building! Located in the Cascade Mountains of Washington state, Mount Rainier is actually a volcano buried under 35 square miles (90.7 sq km) of snow and ice. The mountain, which covers about 100 square miles (259 sq km), reaches a height of 14,410 feet (4,392 m). Its three peaks include Liberty Cap, Point Success, and Columbia Crest. Mt. Rainier National Park was established in 1899.

145

146

World's
COLDEST INHABITED PLACE

Resolute

The residents of RESOLUTE, Canada have to bundle up—the average annual temperature is just -16°F (-26.6°C). Located on the northeast shore of Resolute Bay on the south coast of Cornwallis Island, the community is commonly the starting point for expeditions to the North Pole. In the winter it can stay dark for 24 hours, and in the summer it can stay light during the entire night. Only about 200 people brave the climate year-round, but the area is becoming quite popular with tourists.

WORLD'S COLDEST INHABITED PLACES

Average annual temperature, in degrees Fahrenheit (Celsius)

Resolute, Canada	Oymyakon, Russia	Eureka, Canada	Ostrov Bol'shoy, Russia	Point Barrow, Alaska, USA
-16° (-26.6°)	-6.7° (-21.5°)	5.5° (-14.7°)	9.8° (-12.3°)	10.2° (-12.1°)

World's
HOTTEST INHABITED PLACE

Dallol

Throughout the year, temperatures in DALLOL, Ethiopia, in Africa average 93.2°F (34.0°C). Dallol is at the northernmost tip of the Great Rift Valley. The Dallol Depression reaches 328 feet (100 m) below sea level, making it the lowest point below sea level that is not covered by water. The area also has several active volcanoes. The only people to inhabit the region are the Afar, who have adapted to the harsh conditions there. For instance, to collect water the women build covered stone piles and wait for condensation to form on the rocks.

147

WORLD'S HOTTEST INHABITED PLACES

Average temperature, in degrees Fahrenheit (Celsius)

93.2° (34.0°)

90.9° (32.7°)

89.1° (31.7°)

87.4° (30.7°)

86.8° (30.4°)

| Dallol, Ethiopia | Bangkok, Thailand | Manila, Philippines | Singapore, Singapore | Assab, Eritrea |

World's
WETTEST INHABITED PLACE

Cherrapunji

Each year, some 498 inches (1,265 cm) of rain falls on CHERRAPUNJI, India. That's enough rain to cover a 4-story building! Most of the region's rain falls within a 6-month period, during the monsoon season. It's not uncommon for constant rain to pelt the area for 2 months straight without even a 10-minute break. During the other 6 months, the winds change and carry the rain away from Cherrapunji, leaving the ground dry and dusty. Ironically, this causes a drought throughout most of the area.

WORLD'S WETTEST INHABITED PLACES

Average annual rainfall, in inches (centimeters)

Cherrapunji, India	Mawsynram, India	Waialeale, Hawaii	Debundscha, Cameroon	Quibdo, Colombia
498 (1,265)	467 (1,187)	451 (1,146)	404 (1,026)	353 (897)

148

149

World's
DRIEST INHABITED PLACE

Aswan

Each year, only .02 inches (.5 mm) of rain falls on ASWAN, Egypt. In the country's sunniest and southernmost city, summer temperatures can reach a blistering 114°F (46°C). Aswan is located on the west bank of the Nile River. The Aswan High Dam, at 12,565 feet (3,830 m) long, is the city's most famous landmark. It produces the majority of Egypt's power in the form of hydroelectricity. Aswan also has many Pharaonic, Greco-Roman, and Muslim ruins.

WORLD'S DRIEST INHABITED PLACES

Average annual rainfall, in inches (millimeters)

Aswan, Egypt	0.02 (0.5)
Arica, Chile	0.03 (0.76)
Luxor, Egypt	0.03 (0.76)
Ica, Peru	0.09 (2.3)
Wadi Halfa, Sudan	0.10 (2.5)

150

Place with the
World's

FASTEST WINDS

Mount Washington

The wind gusts at the top of MOUNT WASHINGTON reached 231 miles (372 km) per hour in 1934—and these gusts were not part of a storm. Normally, the average wind speed at the summit of this mountain is approximately 36 miles (58 km) per hour. Located in the White Mountains of New Hampshire, Mount Washington is the highest peak in New England at 6,288 feet (1,917 m). The treeless summit, which is known for its harsh weather, has an average annual temperature of only 26.5° (-3.1°C).

Speed of strongest winds,
in miles (kilometers) per hour

231 (372)	200 (322)	185 (298)	125 (201)	115 (185)
Mount Washington, New Hampshire, USA	Common-wealth Bay, Antarctica	South Pole, Antarctica	New Orleans, Louisiana, USA	Fargo, North Dakota, USA

WORLD'S TALLEST WEEDS

Average height, in feet (meters)

12 (3.6)	9 (2.7)	8.9 (2.7)	7 (2.1)	6 (1.8)
Giant Hogweed	Burdock	Giant Ragweed	Lambs-quarters	Bull Thistle

World's TALLEST WEED

Giant Hogweed

Growing to a height of 12 feet (3.6 m), the GIANT HOGWEED can have leaves that measure 3 feet (91 cm) long. This weed is taller than some trees! The giant hogweed is part of the parsley, or carrot, family and it has hollow stalks with tiny white flowers. Although it was first brought to America from Asia as an ornamental plant, the hogweed quickly became a pest. Each plant can produce about 50,000 seeds and spreads quickly through its environment.

151

PLANTS

152

World's
LARGEST LEAVES

Raffia Palm

The RAFFIA PALM tree has leaves that reach
lengths of 65 feet (19.8 m) long—about the
same length as a regulation tennis court.
Raffia trees have several stems that can reach
heights of 6 to 30 feet (2 to 9 m). When they
reach about 50 years of age, raffia palms flower
and produce egg-size fruits covered in hard
scales. Several products come from these palms,
including raffia, and floor and shoe polish.
Raffia leaves are also used to weave baskets,
mats, and hats. These enormous plants are
native to Madagascar, but most of the native
growth has been overharvested. The palms are
now cultivated in West and East Africa.

WORLD'S LARGEST LEAVES

Length, in feet (meters)

Raffia Palm	Fan Palm	Date Palm	Coconut Palm	Oil Palm
65 (19.8)	20 (6)	18 (5.5)	16 (5)	13 (4)

World's
TALLEST CACTUS

Saguaro

Many SAGUARO cacti grow to a height of 50 feet (15 m), but some have actually reached 75 feet (23 m). That's taller than a 7-story building. Saguaros start out quite small and grow very slowly. A saguaro only reaches about 1 inch (2.5 cm) high during its first 10 years. It will not bloom until it is between 50 and 75 years old. By this time, the cactus has a strong root system that can support about 9 to 10 tons (8 to 9 t) of growth. Its spines can measure up to 2.5 inches (5 cm) long. Saguaro cacti live for about 170 years. The giant cactus can be found from southeastern California to southern Arizona.

153

WORLD'S TALLEST CACTI

Maximum height, in feet (meters)

75 (23)	50 (15)	33 (10)	30 (9)	12 (3.7)
Saguaro	Organ Pipe	Opuntia	Cane Cholla	Barrel

Country that
Produces the

MOST FRUIT

China

Each year, CHINA produces
about 91 million tons (82
million t) of fruit—about
14% of the world's total fruit
production. The country's
fruit crop is worth about $13
billion annually. China is
the world's top producer of
apples and pears, and ranks
third in the world for citrus
fruit production. The country's
orchards total about 21.5
million acres (8.6 million ha)—
almost a quarter of the world's
orchard land. More than half
of China's population works in
the agriculture industry.

154

COUNTRIES THAT PRODUCE THE MOST FRUIT

Millions of tons (metric tons)
produced annually

China	India	Brazil	USA	Mexico
90.9 (82.5)	51.8 (47.0)	39.5 (35.8)	28.7 (26.0)	19.9 (18.0)

155

World's
TALLEST TREE

California Redwood

Growing in both California and southern Oregon, CALIFORNIA REDWOODS can reach a height of 385 feet (117.4 m). Their trunks can grow up to 25 feet (7.6 m) in diameter. The tallest redwood on record stands 385 feet (117.4 m) tall—more than 60 feet (18.3 m) taller than the Statue of Liberty. Amazingly, this giant tree grows from a seed the size of a tomato. Some redwoods are believed to be more than 2,000 years old. The trees' thick bark and foliage protect them from natural hazards such as insects and fires.

WORLD'S TALLEST TREE SPECIES

Maximum height, in feet (meters)

California Redwood	Giant Sequoia	Eucalyptus	Douglas Fir	Japanese Cedar
385 (117)	350 (99)	300 (91)	250 (63)	175 (53)

World's

MOST POISONOUS MUSHROOM

Death Cap

DEATH CAP mushrooms are members of the Amanita family, which are among the most dangerous mushrooms in the world. The death cap contains deadly peptide toxins that cause rapid loss of bodily fluids and intense thirst. Within six hours, the poison shuts down the kidneys, liver, and central nervous system, causing coma and—in more than 50% of cases—death. Estimates of the number of poisonous mushroom species range from 80 to 2,000. Most experts agree, however, that at least 100 varieties will cause severe symptoms and even death if eaten.

156

WORLD'S MOST POISONOUS MUSHROOMS

Risk of fatality if consumed

Extreme	Very High	High	Medium	Low
Death Cap	Destroying Angel	Amanita Alba	Fly Agaric	Deadly Galerina

Maximum flower size, in inches (centimeters)

Rafflesia	Sunflower	Giant Water Lily	Brazilian Dutchman	Magnolia
36 (91)	19 (48)	18 (46)	14 (36)	10 (25)

World's
LARGEST FLOWER

PLANTS

Rafflesia

The blossoms of the giant RAFFLESIA—or "stinking corpse lily"—can reach 36 inches (91 cm) in diameter and weigh up to 25 pounds (11 kg). Its petals can grow 1.5 feet (0.5 m) long and 1 inch (2.5 cm) thick. There are 16 different species of Rafflesia. This endangered plant is found only in the rain forests of Borneo and Sumatra. It lives inside the bark of host vines and is noticeable only when its flowers break through to blossom. The large, reddish-purple flowers give off a smell similar to rotting meat, which attracts insects to help spread the rafflesia's pollen.

157

158

World's
DEADLIEST PLANT

Castor Bean Plant

The CASTOR BEAN PLANT produces seeds that contain a protein called ricin. Scientists estimate that ricin is about 6,000 times more poisonous than cyanide and 12,000 times more poisonous than rattlesnake venom. It would take a particle of ricin only about the size of a grain of sand to kill a 160-pound (73 kg) adult. The deadly beans are actually quite pretty and are sometimes used in jewelry. Castor bean plants grow in warmer climates and can reach a height of about 10 feet (3 m). Its leaves can measure up to 2 feet (0.6 m) wide.

WORLD'S DEADLIEST PLANTS

Risk of fatality if consumed

Extreme	High	High	Medium	Low
Castor Bean	Rosary Bead	Foxglove	Azalea	English Ivy

SOME OF THE WORLD'S LARGEST SEEDS

Length, in inches (centimeters)

12 (30)	6 (15)	3 (7.6)	2 (3)	1 (2.5)
Coco de Mer	Coconut	Avocado	Peach	Acorn

World's LARGEST SEED

Coco de Mer

Measuring 3 feet (1 m) in diameter and 12 inches (30 cm) in length, the giant, dark brown seed of the COCO DE MER palm tree can weigh up to 40 pounds (18 kg). Only a few thousand seeds are produced each year. Coco de mer trees are found on the island of Praslin in the Seychelles Archipelago of the Indian Ocean. The area where some of the few remaining trees grow has been declared a Natural World Heritage Site in an effort to protect the species from poachers looking for the rare seeds. The tree can grow up to 100 feet (31 m) tall, with leaves measuring 20 feet (6 m) long and 12 feet (3.6 m) wide.

World's
HIGHEST TSUNAMI WAVE SINCE 1900

Lituya Bay

A 1,720-foot- (524-m-) high tsunami wave crashed down in LITUYA BAY, Alaska, on July 9, 1958. Located in Glacier Bay National Park, the tsunami was caused by a massive landslide that was triggered by an 8.3 magnitude earthquake. The water from the bay covered 5 square miles (13 sq km) of land and traveled inland as far as 3,600 feet (1,097 m). Millions of trees were washed away. Amazingly, because the area was very isolated and the coastline was sheltered by coves, only two people died when their fishing boat sank.

WORLD'S HIGHEST TSUNAMI WAVES SINCE 1900

Height of wave, in feet (meters)

1,720 (524)	75 (23)	60 (18)	50 (15)	33 (10)
Lituya Bay, Alaska, USA, 1958	Chile, 1960	Philippines, 1960	Southern Asia, 2004	Solomon Islands, 2007

World's
MOST INTENSE EARTHQUAKE SINCE 1900

Coastal Chile

An explosive earthquake measuring 9.5 on the Richter scale rocked the coast of CHILE on May 22, 1960. This is equal to the intensity of about 60,000 hydrogen bombs. Some 2,000 people were killed and another 3,000 injured. The death toll was fairly low because the foreshocks frightened people into the streets. When the massive jolt came, many of the collapsed buildings were already empty. The coastal towns of Valdivia and Puerto Montt suffered the most damage because they were closest to the epicenter—located about 100 miles (161 km) offshore.

WORLD'S MOST INTENSE EARTHQUAKES SINCE 1900

Magnitude

9.5	9.4	9.2	9.0	8.9
Chile, 1960	Indonesia, 1964	Alaska, USA, 1964	Southeast Asia, 2004	Japan, 1933

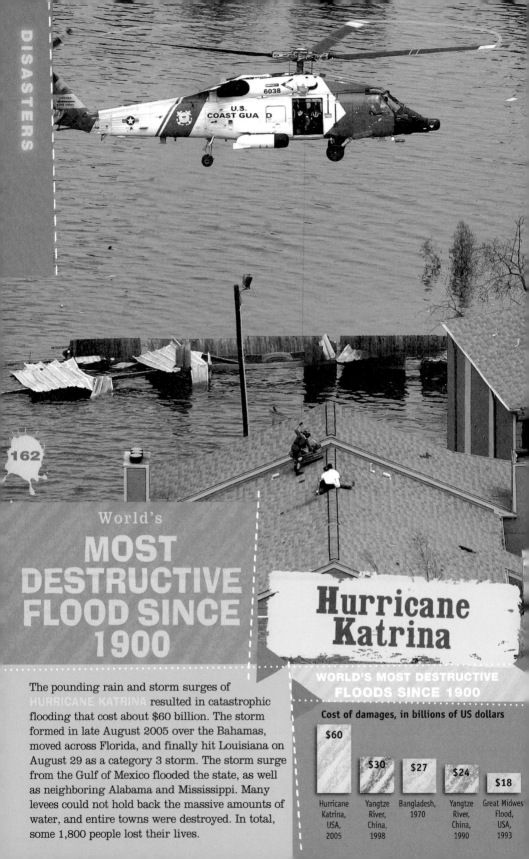

162

World's

MOST DESTRUCTIVE FLOOD SINCE 1900

Hurricane Katrina

The pounding rain and storm surges of HURRICANE KATRINA resulted in catastrophic flooding that cost about $60 billion. The storm formed in late August 2005 over the Bahamas, moved across Florida, and finally hit Louisiana on August 29 as a category 3 storm. The storm surge from the Gulf of Mexico flooded the state, as well as neighboring Alabama and Mississippi. Many levees could not hold back the massive amounts of water, and entire towns were destroyed. In total, some 1,800 people lost their lives.

WORLD'S MOST DESTRUCTIVE FLOODS SINCE 1900

Cost of damages, in billions of US dollars

$60	$30	$27	$24	$18
Hurricane Katrina, USA, 2005	Yangtze River, China, 1998	Bangladesh, 1970	Yangtze River, China, 1990	Great Midwest Flood, USA, 1993

Oil spilled, in tons (metric tons)

220,000 (199,581)	160,000 (145,150)	119,000 (107,955)	85,000 (77,111)	72,000 (65,317)
Amoco Cadiz, Brittany, France 1978	Atlantic Empress, Tobago, 1979	Torrey Canyon, Isles of Scilly, UK, 1967	Braer, Shetland Isles UK, 1993	Sea Empress, Milford Haven, UK, 1996

World's
WORST OIL SPILL

Amoco Cadiz

On March 16, 1978, the AMOCO CADIZ hit ground in shallow water off the coast of Brittany, France and spilled 220,000 tons (199,581 t) of oil into the English Channel. The very large crude carrier encountered strong storms and lost the ability to steer. Tug boats and the ship's anchor were unable to stop the tanker from drifting, and it collided with the rocky shore. The ship's hull and storage tanks were ripped open, and 68.7 million gallons (260 million l) of oil spread across 125 miles (201 km) of the Brittany coastline. The oil slick ruined fisheries, oyster beds, and surrounding beaches.

163

World's
MOST DESTRUCTIVE TORNADO SINCE 1900

Oklahoma City

On May 3, 1999, a devastating tornado swept through downtown OKLAHOMA CITY, Oklahoma, killing 36 people and causing more than $1.2 billion in damages. This powerful twister traveled almost 38 miles (61 km) in four hours and measured a mile (1.6 km) wide at times. With raging winds reaching 318 miles (512 km) per hour, it was the strongest wind speed ever recorded. More than 800 houses were destroyed in Oklahoma City alone. Because of the mass destruction caused by this twister, it was classified as a five—the second-highest possible rating—on the Fujita Tornado Scale.

WORLD'S MOST DESTUCTIVE TORNADOES SINCE 1900

Cost of damages, in US dollars

$1.2 B	$1.1 B	$1.0 B	$650 M	$450 M
Oklahoma City, Oklahoma, 1999	Omaha, Nebraska, 1975	Missouri, Illinois, Indiana, 1925	Southern United States, 2006	Pennsylvania, Ohio, 1985

164

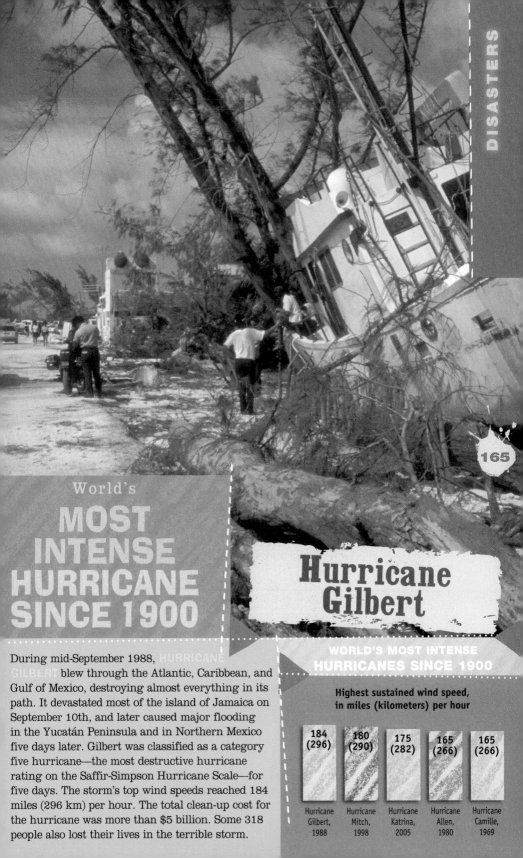

165

World's
MOST INTENSE HURRICANE SINCE 1900

Hurricane Gilbert

During mid-September 1988, HURRICANE GILBERT blew through the Atlantic, Caribbean, and Gulf of Mexico, destroying almost everything in its path. It devastated most of the island of Jamaica on September 10th, and later caused major flooding in the Yucatán Peninsula and in Northern Mexico five days later. Gilbert was classified as a category five hurricane—the most destructive hurricane rating on the Saffir-Simpson Hurricane Scale—for five days. The storm's top wind speeds reached 184 miles (296 km) per hour. The total clean-up cost for the hurricane was more than $5 billion. Some 318 people also lost their lives in the terrible storm.

WORLD'S MOST INTENSE HURRICANES SINCE 1900

Highest sustained wind speed, in miles (kilometers) per hour

Hurricane Gilbert, 1988	Hurricane Mitch, 1998	Hurricane Katrina, 2005	Hurricane Allen, 1980	Hurricane Camille, 1969
184 (296)	180 (290)	175 (282)	165 (266)	165 (266)

Pop Culture Records

Television • Music

Theater • Movies

Books • Art

167

MOST POPULAR TELEVISION SHOW

American Idol Wednesday

AMERICAN IDOL on Wednesday pulled in 17.3% of the viewing audience during the 2007 season. During the sixth season of the wildly popular singing competition, the show's contestants performed in front of judges Simon Cowell, Randy Jackson, and Paula Abdul. Once the field of contestants was narrowed down by the judges, viewers voted Jordin Sparks as the newest American Idol with the majority of the 74 million votes cast. A spin-off of the UK's *Pop Idol*, *American Idol* premiered on Fox in 2002.

MOST POPULAR TELEVISION SHOWS

Average audience percentage in 2007

American Idol Wednesday	American Idol Tuesday	Dancing with the Stars	Dancing with the Stars Monday	Dancing with the Stars Tuesday
17.3	16.8	13.3	12.7	12.6

168

HIGHEST-PAID TV ACTOR

Kiefer Sutherland

KIEFER SUTHERLAND became the highest-paid actor on television when he signed a three-year deal worth $40 million to star in *24*. That averages out to $555,555 per episode! Sutherland plays federal agent Jack Bauer, a crime-fighting hero who battles domestic terrorism. *24* is unique in that every episode in the season portrays one consecutive hour of one day. Since the show began in 2001, Sutherland has won a Golden Globe, an Emmy® Award, and a Screen Actor's Guild Award for his performance.

HIGHEST-PAID TV ACTORS

Money earned per episode during the 2007–2008 season, in US dollars

$555,555	$350,000	$330,000	$325,000	$325,000
Kiefer Sutherland, 24	Charlie Sheen, Two and a Half Men	Chris Meloni, Law & Order: SVU	William Petersen, CSI	Zach Braff, Scrubs

Money earned per episode during the 2007–2008 season, in US dollars

440,000	440,000	440,000	440,000	330,000
Teri Hatcher, *Desperate Housewives*	Marcia Cross, *Desperate Housewives*	Felicity Huffman, *Desperate Housewives*	Eva Longoria, *Desperate Housewives*	Mariska Hargitay, *Law & Order: SVU*

HIGHEST-PAID TV ACTRESS

Desperate Housewives

Marcia Cross, Teri Hatcher, Felicity Huffman, and Eva Longoria—the main cast of the hit show *DESPERATE HOUSEWIVES*—each make $440,000 an episode. The ladies of Wisteria Lane are better known as Bree Van De Kamp (Cross), Susan Mayer (Hatcher), Lynette Scavo (Huffman), and Gabrielle Solis (Longoria) to television audiences. Executive producer Marc Cherry brought this nighttime soap to life in 2004, and since then the show has won six Emmy® Awards and two Golden Globes.

HIGHEST-PAID TALK SHOW HOST

Oprah Winfrey

170

OPRAH WINFREY pulled in $260 million in 2007, making her the world's top-paid entertainer. In total, she is worth more than $1.2 billion. Oprah's self-made millions have come mostly from her television show, which began in 1983. Since then, Oprah has been educating her viewers and helping her audience with tough social issues. The megastar is also involved in movies, television production, magazines, books, radio, and the Internet. Oprah is known for her great generosity, and has donated millions to various charities.

HIGHEST-PAID TALK SHOW HOSTS

Income in 2007, in millions of US dollars

$260	$40	$30	$30	$21
Oprah Winfrey	David Letterman	Dr. Phil McGraw	Judge Judy Sheindlin	Regis Philbin

171

United States'
BESTSELLING MALE RECORDING ARTIST

Garth Brooks

GARTH BROOKS has sold 128 million albums since his professional career began in 1989. Brooks's career skyrocketed in 1991, when his third album—*Ropin' the Wind*—became the first country music album to debut on the top of the pop charts. From 1996 to 1999, Garth's tour stopped at 350 venues in 100 cities. More than 5.3 million tickets were sold, and it is considered one of the most successful tours in history. When the tour finished, Garth released his *Double Live* CD, and it became the bestselling live album ever. In all, Brooks has released 31 albums to date, and won 15 Academy of Country Music Awards.

UNITED STATES' BESTSELLING MALE RECORDING ARTISTS

Albums sold, in millions

Garth Brooks	Elvis Presley	Billy Joel	Elton John	George Strait
128.0	118.5	79.5	69.5	67.0

United States' BESTSELLING FEMALE RECORDING ARTIST

Barbra Streisand

BARBRA STREISAND has sold almost 71 million copies of her work during her 39 years as a singer. She has recorded more than 50 albums and has more gold albums—or albums that have sold at least 500,000 copies—than any other entertainer in history. Streisand has 47 gold albums, 28 platinum albums, and 13 multiplatinum albums. Some of her recordings include "I Finally Found Someone" (1996), "Tell Him" (1997), and "If You Ever Leave Me" (1999). Some of her best-known film work includes roles in *Funny Girl*, *The Way We Were*, *Yentl*, and *Meet the Fockers*. Streisand has won 10 Grammys®, 2 Academy Awards®, 6 Emmy® Awards, and 11 Golden Globes.

172

UNITED STATES' BESTSELLING FEMALE RECORDING ARTISTS

Albums sold, in millions

71.0	63.0	61.5	54.0	49.0
Barbra Streisand	Madonna	Mariah Carey	Whitney Houston	Celine Dion

173

World's
TOP-EARNING MALE SINGER

Justin Timberlake

Thanks to an extremely popular second solo album and very successful tour, JUSTIN TIMBERLAKE earned $126 million in 2007. He co-wrote and co-produced the album, which has already sold more than 4 million copies. The former Mickey Mouse Club star has ventured into acting as well, appearing in *Alpha Dog* and *The Love Guru*. Timberlake also starred in a Pepsi commercial that aired during the 2008 Super Bowl. He won four MTV Video Music Awards and was nominated for Best Male Artist at the American Music Awards in 2007.

WORLD'S TOP-EARNING MALE SINGERS OF 2007

Income, in millions of US dollars

$126	$83	$71	$70	$53
Justin Timberlake	Jay-Z	Kenny Chesney	Rod Stewart	Elton John

World's
TOP-EARNING FEMALE SINGER

Madonna

Music legend MADONNA made $72 million in 2007 from album sales and concert ticket sales. Her Confessions Tour played 61 shows in 12 countries. Madonna is also a children's book author, selling more than 3 million books from her English Roses series. She also launched a clothing line with H&M called "M." During her career, she has earned 7 Grammy® Awards. In March 2008, Madonna was inducted into the Rock & Roll Hall of Fame, exactly 25 years after the release of her first album.

WORLD'S TOP-EARNING FEMALE SINGERS OF 2007

Income, in millions of US dollars

Madonna	Celine Dion	Miley Cyrus	Beyoncé	Gwen Stefani
$72	$45	$37	$19	$16

United States' BESTSELLING RECORDING GROUP

MUSIC

Millions of albums sold

170.0	111.5	98.0	74.5	69.0
The Beatles	Led Zeppelin	The Eagles	Pink Floyd	AC/DC

The Beatles

THE BEATLES have sold 170 million copies of their albums in the United States since their first official recording session in September 1962. In the two years that followed, they had 26 Top 40 singles. John Lennon, Paul McCartney, George Harrison, and Ringo Starr made up the "Fab Four," as the Beatles were known. Together they recorded many albums that are now considered rock masterpieces, such as *Rubber Soul*, *Sgt. Pepper's Lonely Hearts Club Band*, and *The Beatles*. The group broke up in 1969. In 2001, however, their newly released greatest hits album—*The Beatles 1*—reached the top of the charts. One of their best-known songs—"Yesterday"—is the most recorded song in history, with about 2,500 different artists recording their own versions.

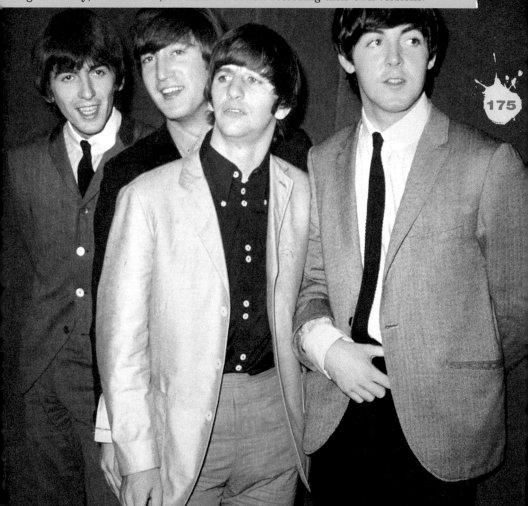

175

Male Singer with the MOST MULTI-PLATINUM ALBUMS

Elvis Presley

ELVIS PRESLEY made 24 albums that have achieved multiplatinum status. An album has to sell more than a million copies to be considered platinum, and an additional million or more to be multiplatinum. Some of Elvis's most successful albums include *Elvis' Christmas Album* (9 times platinum), *Elvis' Golden Records* (6 times platinum), and *Aloha from Hawaii* (5 times platinum). In fact, there are 150 Elvis songs and albums that have been certified as gold, platinum, or multiplatinum in the United States.

MALE SINGERS WITH THE MOST MULTIPLATINUM ALBUMS

Number of albums

Elvis	Garth Brooks	George Strait	Elton John	Billy Joe
24	15	13	12	12

177

Female Singer with the MOST MULTI-PLATINUM ALBUMS

Barbra Streisand

BARBRA STREISAND has a total of 13 albums that are certified multiplatinum. Some of Streisand's most successful albums are *Guilty* (5 times platinum), *A Christmas Album* (5 times platinum), *The Broadway Album* (4 times platinum), and *A Star Is Born* (4 times platinum). She is also the only recording artist to achieve a number-one Billboard album in four consecutive decades, beginning in 1960. And on December 31, 1999, Streisand made history when her concert at the MGM Grand grossed more than $14.7 million.

FEMALE SINGERS WITH THE MOST MULTIPLATINUM ALBUMS

Number of albums

Barbra Streisand	Madonna	Reba McIntyre	Linda Rondstadt	Anne Murray
13	12	9	7	2

178

World's
TOP-EARNING BAND

The Police

THE POLICE launched a reunion tour in 2007 that grossed $212 million. This is the first time the band has played in concert together since 1986. The band, which consists of lead singer Sting, drummer Stewart Copeland, and guitarist Andy Summers, sold more than 1.8 million tickets. Some of the band's most well-known songs include "Roxanne," "Message in a Bottle," and "Don't Stand So Close To Me." The Police were inducted into the Rock & Roll Hall of Fame in 2003.

WORLD'S TOP-EARNING BANDS OF 2007

Earnings, in millions of US dollars

$212 — The Police
$129 — Genesis
$88 — The Rolling Stones
$67 — Bon Jovi
$30 — U2

ACTS WITH THE MOST COUNTRY MUSIC AWARDS

Number of awards

20	19	16	11	10
Brooks & Dunn	Vince Gill	Alan Jackson	Garth Brooks	Dixie Chicks

Act with the MOST COUNTRY MUSIC AWARDS

Brooks & Dunn

Kix Brooks and Ronnie Dunn, the duo that makes up BROOKS & DUNN, have won 20 Country Music Association Awards since they began singing together in 1990. The pair has sold more than 30 million albums and had 23 number-one hits. Some of their most successful songs include "Brand New Man," "Boot Scootin' Boogie," "You're Gonna Miss Me When I'm Gone," and "Red Dirt Road." They also hold the record for the most Academy of Country Music Awards, with 26 wins.

179

Play with the

MOST TONY AWARDS®

The Producers

In March 2001, *THE PRODUCERS* took home 12 of its record-breaking 15 Tony Award® nominations. The Broadway smash won awards for Best Musical, Best Original Score, Best Book, Best Direction of a Musical, Best Choreography, Best Orchestration, Best Scenic Design, Best Costume Design, Best Lighting Design, Best Actor in a Musical, Best Featured Actor in a Musical, and Best Actress in a Musical. *The Producers,* which originally starred Nathan Lane and Matthew Broderick, is a stage adaptation of Mel Brooks's 1968 movie. Brooks wrote the lyrics and music for 16 new songs for the stage version.

PLAYS WITH THE MOST TONY AWARDS®

Number of Tony Awards®

12	10	8	8	7
The Producers, 2001	Hello, Dolly!, 1964	Spring Awakening, 2007	The Phantom of the Opera, 1988	The Coast of Utopia, 2007

181

World's LONGEST-RUNNING BROADWAY SHOW

The Phantom of the Opera

THE PHANTOM OF THE OPERA has been performed more than 8,343 times since the show opened in January 1988. The show tells the story of a disfigured musical genius who terrorizes the performers of the Paris Opera House. More than 80 million people have seen a performance, and box-office receipts total more than $3.2 billion. The show won 7 Tony Awards® its opening year, including Best Musical. The musical drama is performed at the Majestic Theatre.

WORLD'S LONGEST-RUNNING BROADWAY SHOWS

Total performances*

8,343	7,485	6,680	6,137	5,959
The Phantom of the Opera, 1988-	Cats, 1982-2000	Les Misérables, 1982-2000	A Chorus Line, 1975-1990	Oh! Calcutta!, 1969-1972

*As of February 23, 2008

182

Actor with the

HIGHEST CAREER BOX-OFFICE EARNINGS

Frank Welker

FRANK WELKER's movies have a combined total gross of $4.99 billion. Although movie fans might not recognize Welker's name or face, they would probably recognize one of his voices. Welker is a voice actor, and has worked on 89 movies in the last 25 years. Some of his most famous voices include Megatron, Curious George, and Scooby-Doo. Some of Welker's most profitable movies include *How the Grinch Stole Christmas, Godzilla,* and *101 Dalmatians.*

ACTORS WITH THE HIGHEST CAREER BOX-OFFICE EARNINGS

Earnings, in billions of US dollars*

$4.99

$4.00

$3.83

$3.44

$3.30

| Frank Welker | Samuel L. Jackson | Tom Hanks | Eddie Murphy | Harrison Ford |

*As of February 23, 2008

WORLD'S TOP-GROSSING KIDS' MOVIES

Box-office receipts, in US dollars

$1.04 B — Snow White and the Seven Dwarfs, 1937

$977 M — Harry Potter and the Sorcerer's Stone, 2001

$938 M — Harry Potter and the Order of the Phoenix, 2007

$915 M — Shrek 2, 2004

$896 M — Harry Potter and the Goblet of Fire, 2005

World's TOP-GROSSING KIDS' MOVIE

Snow White and the Seven Dwarfs

Walt Disney's SNOW WHITE AND THE SEVEN DWARFS has earned an amazing $1.04 billion in box-office receipts in the 69 years since its debut. (To compare the success of films throughout the decades, it is necessary to adjust for inflation.) More than 750 artists contributed during the three-year production. *Snow White and the Seven Dwarfs* was the first-ever animated feature film, and it cost $1.4 million to make. Many of the songs in the movie, including "Some Day My Prince Will Come" and "Whistle While You Work," have become true American classics.

183

THE BATTLE WITHIN.

MOVIES

184

Movie with the
MOST SUCCESSFUL OPENING WEEKEND

Spider-Man 3

SPIDER-MAN 3 opened on May 4, 2007 with box-office receipts totaling $151.2 million. The film sold 22.4 million tickets in North America alone in one day. The third installment of this comic book blockbuster features Peter Parker (Tobey Maguire) and his girlfriend Mary Jane Watson (Kirsten Dunst) saving New York City from evil. This time, the villains include the Sandman (Thomas Hayden Church), Venom (Topher Grace), and the New Goblin (James Franco). However, Spider-Man also has to battle the evil within himself when an alien symbiote turns his suit black.

MOVIES WITH THE MOST SUCCESSFUL OPENING WEEKENDS

Weekend earnings, in millions of US dollars

$151.2	$135.6	$121.6	$121.6	$114.7
Spider-Man 3, 5/4/07	Pirates of the Caribbean: Dead Man's Chest, 7/7/06	Spider-Man, 5/3/02	Shrek the Third, 5/18/07	Pirates of the Caribbean: At World's End, 5/25/07

Movies with the
MOST OSCARS®

Ben-Hur, The Lord of the Rings: The Return of the King, & Titanic

The only three films in Hollywood history to win 11 Academy Awards® are BEN-HUR, THE LORD OF THE RINGS: THE RETURN OF THE KING, and TITANIC. Some of the Oscar® wins for *Ben-Hur*—a biblical epic based on an 1880 novel by General Lew Wallace—include Best Actor (Charlton Heston) and Director (William Wyler). *The Lord of the Rings: The Return of the King* is the final film in the epic trilogy based on the works of J.R.R. Tolkien. With 11 awards, it is the most successful movie in Academy Awards® history because it won in every category in which it was nominated. Some of these wins include Best Picture, Director (Peter Jackson), and Costume Design. Some of *Titanic's* Oscars® include Best Cinematography, Visual Effects, and Costume Design.

MOVIES WITH THE MOST OSCAR® WINS

Oscars® won

11	11	11	10	9
Ben-Hur, 1959	Titanic, 1997	The Lord of the Rings: The Return of the King, 2004	West Side Story, 1961	The Last Emperor, 1987

186

TOP MOVIE-GOING COUNTRY

USA

AMERICAN movie-goers spend more than $9.4 billion on trips to the big screen. The average American sees about 6 movies annually. That equals about 1.55 billion admissions annually, with an average ticket price of $6.88. Some 475 movies are released throughout the country each year. When a new movie is released, it runs for about eight weeks in theaters and is shown on about 2,000 screens.

TOP MOVIE-GOING COUNTRIES

2007 Box Office Revenue in 2007, in billions of US dollars

USA	Japan	UK	France	Germany
9.42	1.84	1.39	1.39	1.02

COUNTRIES WITH THE MOST MOVIE SCREENS

Number of movie screens

Country	Number of movie screens
USA	38,852
India	10,500
France	5,366
Germany	4,889
China	3,034

Country with the

MOST MOVIE SCREENS

United States

There are about 38,852 movie screens located in 35,000 movie theaters throughout the UNITED STATES. Since the first permanent electric theater opened in 1902, Americans have flocked to the big screen. Megaplexes, or large movie theaters that show several movies at the same time, are the most popular type of theater in the country. Approximately 1.2 billion movie tickets are sold in the United States each year, with an average price of $6.88.

187

HIGHEST ANIMATED FILM BUDGET

The Polar Express

THE POLAR EXPRESS went into production with an unprecedented budget of $150 million. Its final production cost totaled $170 million. The film used new computer-generated technology called performance capture, giving the animation an incredibly realistic look. The animated film is based on the popular children's book about a magical train headed toward the North Pole on Christmas Eve. Several characters in the movie are voiced by Tom Hanks. The film has made more than $150 million since its release in 2004.

MOST POPULAR
TELEVISION SHOWS

HIGHEST ANIMATED FILM BUDGETS

Budget, in millions of US dollars

$170	$145	$143	$140	$137
The Polar Express, 2004	Tarzan, 1999	Flushed Away, 2006	Treasure Planet, 2002	Final Fantasy: The Spirits Within, 2001

188

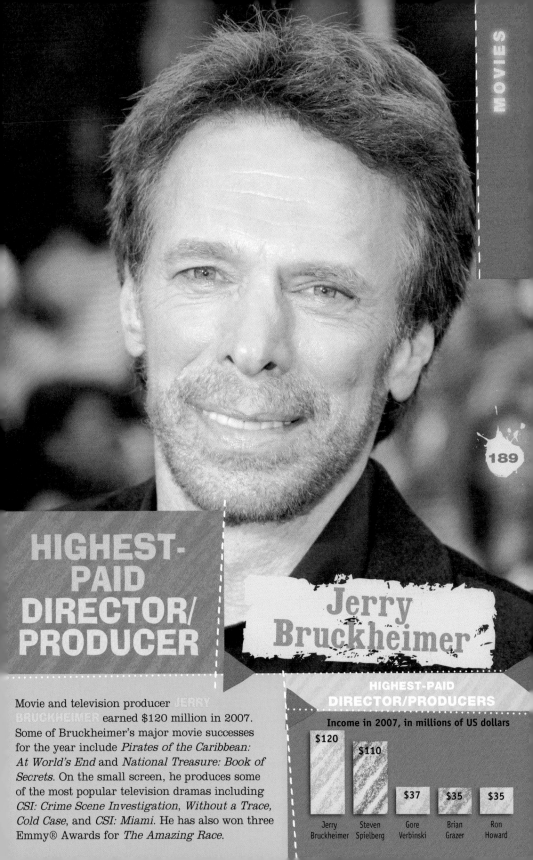

189

HIGHEST-PAID DIRECTOR/ PRODUCER

Jerry Bruckheimer

Movie and television producer JERRY BRUCKHEIMER earned $120 million in 2007. Some of Bruckheimer's major movie successes for the year include *Pirates of the Caribbean: At World's End* and *National Treasure: Book of Secrets*. On the small screen, he produces some of the most popular television dramas including *CSI: Crime Scene Investigation*, *Without a Trace*, *Cold Case*, and *CSI: Miami*. He has also won three Emmy® Awards for *The Amazing Race*.

HIGHEST-PAID DIRECTOR/PRODUCERS

Income in 2007, in millions of US dollars

Jerry Bruckheimer	Steven Spielberg	Gore Verbinski	Brian Grazer	Ron Howard
$120	$110	$37	$35	$35

190

World's
TOP-EARNING ACTOR

Johnny Depp

Thanks mostly to the super-successful *Pirates of the Caribbean* trilogy, JOHNNY DEPP raked in $92 million in 2007. Even though only one of the movies—*At World's End*—came out in 2007, Depp earns a percentage of the profits on all DVD sales and merchandise that continues to sell for the first two Pirates films. The quirky actor's role as Captain Jack Sparrow earned him five People's Choice Awards, Four Teen Choice Awards, two MTV Movie Awards, and 1 Kid's Choice Award. Depp also starred in *Sweeney Todd: The Demon Barber of Fleet Street* in 2007, which earned him an Oscar® nomination and a Golden Globe win.

WORLD'S TOP-EARNING ACTORS

2007 earnings, in millions of US dollars

Johnny Depp	Tom Hanks	Ben Stiller	Brad Pitt	Tom Cruise
$92	$74	$38	$34	$31

World's TOP-EARNING ACTRESS

Nicole Kidman

191

NICOLE KIDMAN was extremely busy in 2007! The Australian movie star turned out three movies, including *The Golden Compass*, *Margot at the Wedding*, and *The Invasion*. So far, the combined worldwide gross of these movies totals more than $406.7 million. And producers know Kidman is a bankable star, with her career box office earnings totaling $3 billion. Kidman, who is married to country singer Keith Urban, has another important project due in 2008—the arrival of her first child.

WORLD'S TOP-EARNING ACTRESSES

2007 earnings, in millions of US dollars

Nicole Kidman	Angelina Jolie	Jennifer Aniston	Julia Roberts	Sandra Bullock
$28	$20	$14	$10	$10

192

World's
TOP-GROSSING MOVIE

Titanic

Directed by James Cameron in 1997, *TITANIC* has grossed more than $600 million in the United States and more than $1.8 billion worldwide. This action-packed drama/romance is set aboard the White Star Line's lavish *RMS Titanic* in 1912. The two main characters, wealthy Rose DeWitt Bukater and poor immigrant Jack Dawson—played by Kate Winslet and Leonardo DiCaprio—meet, and fall in love, before the *Titanic* struck an iceberg on the night of April 14, 1912 and sank into the North Atlantic.

WORLD'S TOP-GROSSING MOVIES

Gross income, in US dollars

$1.85 B	$1.13 B	$1.07 B	$977 M	$952 M
Titanic, 1997	The Lord of the Rings: The Return of the King, 2003	Pirates of the Caribbean: Dead Man's Chest, 2006	Harry Potter and the Sorcerer's Stone, 2001	Pirates of the Caribbean: A World's End 2007

With a budget of $300 million, the PIRATES OF THE CARIBBEAN: AT WORLD'S END creators approved the highest spending in movie history. And all of that money seems to have paid off. The third installment of the Pirates trilogy opened in May 2007 and has since earned more than $960 million worldwide. It is the fifth-highest grossing movie worldwide, and was the fourth-highest domestic gross in 2007. The Jerry Bruckheimer blockbuster starred Johnny Depp as Captain Jack Sparrow, Orlando Bloom as Will Turner, and Keira Knightley as Elizabeth Swann.

World's
LARGEST MOVIE BUDGET

Pirates of the Caribbean: At World's End

WORLD'S LARGEST MOVIE BUDGETS

Budget, in millions of US dollars

$300	$270	$258	$225	$210
Pirates of the Caribbean: At World's End, 2007	Superman Returns, 2006	Spider-Man 3, 2007	Pirates of the Caribbean: Dead Man's Chest, 2006	X-Men: The Last Stand, 2006

World's
MOST SUCESSFUL ARTIST

Pablo Picasso

PABLO PICASSO's work has earned more than $1.399 billion through sales and auctions. In fact, one of the most expensive paintings ever sold was Picasso's "Boy with a Pipe," which brought in $104 million in 2004. The Spanish painter lived from 1881 to 1973. Most of Picasso's career is divided into periods according to the colors and styles he used. First came his Blue Period (1901 to 1904), followed by his Rose Period (1905 to 1907), then his African-influenced period (1908 to 1909), leading to his Analytic Cubism Period (1909 to 1912), and finally his Synthetic Cubism Period (1912 to 1919).

WORLD'S MOST SUCCESSFUL ARTISTS

Total value of work, in of US dollars

Pablo Picasso	Claude Monet	Pierre-Auguste Renoir	Vincent van Gogh	Paul Cézanne
$1.399 B	$1.016 B	$644 M	$552 M	$486 M

194

Money Records

Industry

Wealth

Most Valuable

World's
TOP-SELLING CAR

Toyota Camry

The TOYOTA CAMRY was the most popular car in 2007, with sales totaling almost 430,500 vehicles. The Camry has a standard 2.4-liter, 16-valve engine and features cruise control, keyless entry, and a state-of-the-art audio system. The Camry has also been rated as one of the safest cars on the road. In addition to front, overhead, and side-impact airbags, the car features Vehicle Skid Control brakes.

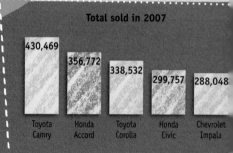

WORLD'S TOP-SELLING CARS

Total sold in 2007

Toyota Camry	Honda Accord	Toyota Corolla	Honda Civic	Chevrolet Impala
430,469	356,772	338,532	299,757	288,048

196

197

World's
MOST PROFITABLE COMPANY

ExxonMobil

Gasoline giant EXXONMOBIL made a ton of cash in 2007, raking in more than $39.5 billion. The company recorded some $335 billion in sales. ExxonMobil produces, transports, and sells crude oil and natural gas worldwide. They also manufacture and sell petroleum products across the globe. In addition, Mobil 1 is the world's most successful motor oil. ExxonMobil has 40 oil refineries in 20 countries and is capable of producing 6.4 million barrels of oil each day. They provide fuel to about 35,000 service stations, some 700 airports, and more than 200 ports.

WORLD'S MOST PROFITABLE COMPANIES

2007 profits, in billions of US dollars

ExxonMobil, USA	UAL, USA	Citigroup, USA	Bank of America, USA	General Electric, USA
$39.5	$22.9	$21.5	$21.1	$20.8

World's
MOST VALUABLE BRAND

Coca-Cola

198

COCA-COLA is worth more money than any other brand in the world, with a company value of $67 billion. Coca-Cola is the largest nonalcoholic beverage company in the world, employing about 55,000 people. Besides soda, the company also produces water, juice, coffee, tea, and sports drinks. In fact, the company has more than 2,400 beverage products. They are ranked first in soda and juice sales, and second in sports drink sales. Coca-Cola products are sold in more than 200 countries.

WORLD'S MOST VALUABLE BRANDS

Brand value, in billions of US dollars

Coca-Cola	Microsoft	IBM	General Electric	Intel
$67.0	$56.9	$56.2	$48.9	$32.3

199

Country that
Spends the
MOST
ON TOYS

United States

**COUNTRIES THAT SPEND
THE MOST ON TOYS**

The toy industry is booming in the UNITED
STATES. In 2007, Americans spent an amazing
$36.5 billion on toys! That's equivalent to every
single person in the country buying $121
worth of toys. It's not too much of a surprise
considering toys are sold practically everywhere,
from grocery stores to hardware stores.
Amazingly, November and December account
for about 40% of the total toy sales for the year.
The United States also leads the world in toy
development, marketing, and advertising, and
employs more than 32,000 people in those fields.

Total spending, in billions of US dollars

$36.5				
	$9.1	$8.9	$6.2	$4.5
USA	China	UK	France	Japan

World's BESTSELLING CANDY BRAND

Hershey's Chocolate Bar

HERSHEY'S CHOCOLATE BAR is the king of the candy world with 9.5% of the market share. Americans eat almost 33 million of these tasty treats each month—the same number of bars it takes to stretch from New York City to Los Angeles. In 1900, Milton Hershey developed a delicious recipe for milk chocolate and turned it into his famous candy bar by 1905. Hershey built what has turned into the largest chocolate factory in the world in Pennsylvania, close to dairy farms and fresh milk. Visitors can tour one of the chocolate-making facilities in Hershey, PA, today to see how the creamy confection turns into bars and Kisses.

WORLD'S BESTSELLING CANDY BRANDS

Percentage of market share

Hershey's Chocolate Bar	M&M's	Reese's Peanut Butter Cups	Snickers	Hershey's Kisses
9.5	9.4	8.6	8.0	7.8

200

201

World's
LARGEST INTERNATIONAL FOOD FRANCHISE

McDonald's

Serving customers in 119 different countries, there are more than 31,100 MCDONALD'S restaurants in the world. The company adds approximately 100 new franchises each year. About 70% of the restaurant franchises are run by local businesspeople. McDonald's serves about 52 million customers each day, about 23 million of whom are in the United States. Out of respect for local cultures, restaurants in different countries modify their menus according to religious or cultural traditions. For example, there is a kosher McDonald's in Jerusalem, and the Big Macs in India are made with lamb instead of beef.

WORLD'S LARGEST INTERNATIONAL FOOD FRANCHISES

Number of franchises

McDonald's	Subway	KFC	Burger King	Pizza Hut
31,177	29,186	14,174	11,407	11,363

World's
RICHEST WOMAN

Liliane Bettencourt

LILIANE BETTENCOURT is the richest woman in the world with $22.9 billion. She is the only daughter of Eugene Schueller, founder of the cosmetic giant L'Oréal. In 1957, Bettencourt inherited her father's money, in addition to a controlling stake in the business. Today, L'Oréal is one of the world's most profitable cosmetics companies. A native of France, Bettencourt is the country's second-richest citizen. She has founded the Bettencourt Schueller Foundation, which grants European scientists $300,000 for research in biology or medicine.

WORLD'S RICHEST WOMEN

Assets, in billions of US dollars

Liliane Bettencourt, France	Christy Walton, USA	Alice L. Walton, USA	Abigail Johnson, USA	Jacqueline Mars, USA
$22.9	$19.2	$19.0	$15.0	$14.0

World's
RICHEST MAN

Warren Buffet

With an estimated fortune totaling $62 billion, WARREN BUFFET is the king of the world's billionaires. His net worth jumped up $10 billion in just one year. The self-made billionaire earned most of his fortune from his soaring Berkshire Hathaway stock, which rose 25% during 2007. The company manages many successful subsidiaries, including Borsheims Fine Jewelry, Dairy Queen, and Geico Auto Insurance. Buffet believes in sharing his wealth and has promised to give 5% of his stock to charity each year. This will total more than $31 billion, and most is going to the Bill & Melinda Gates Foundation.

203

WORLD'S RICHEST MEN

Assets, in billions of US dollars

$62	$60	$58	$45	$43
Warren Buffet, USA	Carlos Slim Helú, Mexico	Bill Gates, USA	Lakshmi Mittal, India	Mukesh Ambani, India

World's
POOREST COUNTRY

Somalia

In SOMALIA—a small country in Eastern Africa—the gross domestic product is just $600 per capita. The country's severe political conflicts make it hard for its inhabitants to earn a living. Agriculture is the most important source of income and accounts for about 40% of the gross domestic profit. Industry and service are also a small source of income. At the end of 2004, the country was hit by a tsunami, which destroyed coastal areas. Approximately 43,000 people in the country are infected with HIV/AIDS, and the life expectancy is just 48 years.

WORLD'S POOREST COUNTRIES

Gross domestic product per capita, in US dollars*

$600	$700	$700	$800	$800
Somalia	Ethiopia	Malawi	Burundi	Timor-Leste

*Calculated by dividing the annual worth of all the goods and services produced in a country by the country's population.

205

World's
RICHEST COUNTRY

Luxembourg

Located in western Europe, the very small country of LUXEMBOURG has a population of 480,000. It has a gross domestic product of $80,800 per person. Luxembourg's low inflation and low unemployment rates help to keep the economy solid. Industry makes up a large part of the country's gross domestic product and includes products such as iron and steel, chemicals, metal products, tires, glass, and aluminum. The country's banking community also plays a significant role in the economy, accounting for about 28% of the gross domestic product.

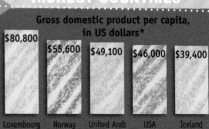

WORLD'S RICHEST COUNTRIES

Gross domestic product per capita, in US dollars*

Luxembourg	Norway	United Arab Emirates	USA	Iceland
$80,800	$55,600	$49,100	$46,000	$39,400

*Calculated by dividing the annual worth of all the goods and services produced in a country by the country's population.

World's
YOUNGEST BILLIONAIRE

Athina Onassis Roussel

Greek shipping tycoon Aristotle Onassis left his granddaughter well provided for. When ATHINA ONASSIS ROUSSEL turned 18 years old in 2003, she inherited an estimated $2.7 billion in properties, including an island in the Ionian Sea, companies, artwork, and a private jet.

At 21, she became president of the Athens-based Onassis Foundation and received another $2 billion. She became the only heir to the Onassis shipping fortune when her mother, Christina, died in 1988. Currently, the estate is being managed by financial advisers. Athina married Brazilian professional equestrian show jumper Alvaro de Miranda Neto in December 2005, and the two reside in Brazil.

WORLD'S YOUNGEST BILLIONAIRES

Age in 2009

Athina Onassis Roussel	Hind Hariri	Albert von Thurn und Taxis	Fahd Hariri	Ayman Hariri
24	25	25	28	30

207

World's MOST EXPENSIVE HOTEL SUITES

The Hardwood Suite & The Atlantis Bridge Suite

The HARDWOOD SUITE at The Palms in Las Vegas and the ATLANTIS BRIDGE SUITE in the Bahamas are the world's most elite vacation destinations. A one-night stay in one of these fancy hotel suites is a whopping $25,000. The Hardwood Suite is a basketball fan's ultimate dream, with a half-court, professional locker room, and scoreboard in the 10,000-square foot suite. Also included in the pricey palace are two master bedrooms, pool tables, plasma TVs, and a media room with a PS2. At the Atlantis Bridge, vacationers relax in a ten-room suite set atop the bridge between the hotel's two towers. The suite also comes with two master bedrooms, marble baths, and an entertainment center, as well as a butler and cook.

WORLD'S MOST EXPENSIVE HOTELS

Price per night, in US dollars

The Palms Fantasy Suites, USA	The Atlantis Resort, Bahamas	President Wilson Hotel, Switzerland	Badrutt's Palace, St. Moritz	Mandarin Oriental, USA
$25,000	$25,000	$23,000	$16,700	$15,000

World's
MOST EXPENSIVE WATCH

Vacheron Constantin Tour de l'Ile

With a ticket price of $1.5 million, the TOUR DE L'ILE is the most valuable watch in the world. It was created by Vacheron Constantin—the world's oldest watchmaker. The piece was made to mark the watchmaker's 250th anniversary. It took 7 years to develop the watch, and an additional 3 years to assemble it. The watch has 834 separate parts, making it the world's most complicated timepiece. Some of the features of the Tour de l'Ile include a perpetual calendar, a moon-phase chart, a sky chart, and the sunrise and sunset times. Only 7 of these luxury watches were made.

208

WORLD'S
MOST EXPENSIVE WATCHES

Price, in US dollars

$1.5 M	$1.1 M	$839,000	$532,000	$477,000
Tour de l'Ile	Chopard Super Ice Cube	Blancpain 1735	Girard-Perregaux Opera Three	Parmigiani Fleurier Toric Corrector Quantième Perpétual

209

United States'
MOST VALUABLE MOVIE FRANCHISE

James Bond

With 22 movies in the franchise, JAMES BOND has brought in almost $4.5 billion throughout the world. The first Bond movie—*Dr. No*—was released in May 1963 with a $1 million budget and earned $59.5 million. The latest and most successful Bond movie—*Casino Royale*—opened in November 2006 with a $102 million budget and has earned $594 million worldwide. A total of $1.08 billion was spent making all of the movies in the franchise, but they have collectively earned more than $4.49 billion. Some of the actors who have played 007 include Sean Connery, Roger Moore, Pierce Brosnan, and Daniel Craig.

UNITED STATES' MOST VALUABLE MOVIE FRANCHISES

Lifetime domestic gross, in billions of US dollars adjusted for inflation

James Bond	Harry Potter	Star Wars	The Lord of the Rings	Pirates of the Caribbean
$4.49	$4.48	$4.34	$2.98	$2.67

World's
MOST EXPENSIVE RESTAURANT

Masa

At this elegant Japanese restaurant, diners will enjoy a meal with an average cost of $400. Located in the Time Warner Building, MASA has just 26 seats. There are no menus here because the sushi chef—Masayoshi Takayama—prepares only what specialties are in season. Diners start with 5 appetizers, followed by a sushi entrée with at least 15 different types of seafood flown in from Japan. Masa opened in 2004 and serves lunch and dinner. If restaurant-goers would like to save a little money, Bar Masa is located next door and offers much more economical meals.

WORLD'S MOST EXPENSIVE RESTAURANTS

Average cost of a meal, in US dollars

$400	$277	$254	$213	$211
Masa, New York City	Aragawa, Tokyo	The French Laundry, Yountville, CA	Eigensinn Farm, Toronto	Arpège, Paris

211

World's
MOST VALUABLE BASEBALL

Mark McGwire's 70th Home-Run Baseball

MARK McGWIRE'S 70th home-run baseball fetched $3.05 million at auction in January 1999. The bid, which was actually $2.7 million plus a large commission fee, is the most money paid for a sports artifact. The ball was only expected to sell for about $1 million. Businessman and baseball fan Todd McFarlane said he bought the ball because he wanted to own a piece of history. This famous baseball marked the end of the exciting 1998 home run race between Mark McGwire and Sammy Sosa. Both beat Roger Maris's three-decade record of 61—Sosa with 66 and McGwire with 70.

WORLD'S MOST VALUABLE BASEBALLS

Price paid at auction, in US dollars

$3.05 M				
	$517,500	$150,000	$125,500	$106,600
McGwire's 70th Home-Run Baseball	Bonds's 73rd Home-Run Baseball	Sosa's 66th Home-Run Baseball	Ruth's First Yankee Stadium Home-Run Baseball	Cubs' 2003 Playoffs Foul Ball

World's
MOST VALUABLE PRODUCTION CAR

Bugatti Veyron 16.4

Volkswagen's BUGATTI VEYRON has a price tag of $1.7 million. That's just slightly less than buying a private jet! The Veyron is also one of the world's fastest cars. With a top speed of 253 miles (407.2 km) per hour, the Veyron can accelerate from 0 to 124 miles (199.6 km) per hour in just 7.3 seconds. Only 300 of these luxury vehicles are produced annually. However, sales have slowed in the last year, and half of the vehicles were not sold. This is most likely due to the sluggish economy and rising fuel prices.

WORLD'S MOST VALUABLE PRODUCTION CARS

Base price, in US dollars

Bugatti Veyron 16.4	Lamborghini Reventon	Ferrari Enzo	SSC Ultimate Aero	Ferrari F50
$1.7 M	$1.4 M	$1.0 M	$600,000	$510,000

212

Science Records

Computers • Technology

Space • Video Games

Vehicles

214

World's
MOST-VISITED WEB SITE

Yahoo! Sites

WEB SITES WITH THE MOST VISITORS

Each month, approximately 133.4 million different people visit a YAHOO! SITE at least once while surfing the Internet. That's more than the entire population of Japan! Yahoo! is the world's largest online community and has more than 500 million users across the globe. In fact, if Yahoo! users joined hands to form a chain, they would circle Earth 11 times. Yahoo! was founded by Jerry Yang and David Filo in 1994. The company's headquarters is located in California, and there are more than 20 offices worldwide.

Number of new users each month, in millions

133.4	123.9	123.7	118.2	81.2
Yahoo! sites	Google sites	Time Warner network	Microsoft sites	Fox Interactive Media

Country with the

MOST INTERNET USERS

United States

The number of Internet users has doubled in the last 5 years. Americans now account for 17% of users worldwide. In the UNITED STATES, more than 210 million people are surfing the World Wide Web. That's more than 50% of the population. Throughout the nation, the largest number of Internet users are women between the ages of 18 and 54, closely followed by men in that age group. Teens, ages 12 to 17, are the third-largest Internet-using group. The average Internet user spends about 14 hours online per week.

215

COUNTRIES WITH THE MOST INTERNET USERS

Users, in millions

210.2	131.1	90.9	67.6	50.3
USA	China	Japan	India	Germany

World's
FASTEST
COMPUTER

Blue Gene

BLUE GENE is the most powerful supercomputer in the world and is capable of performing 478.2 trillion calculations per second. That's about the same as every person in the world doing 72,430 calculations in a second. Housed in the Lawrence Livermore National Laboratory in California, Blue Gene is made up of 131,000 processors and is almost 3 times faster than the next-fastest computer. Blue Gene is used by the government to study classified information.

216

WORLD'S
FASTEST COMPUTERS

Calculations per second, in trillions

478.2	167.3	126.9	117.9	102.8
Blue Gene	JUGENE	SGI Altix ICE 8200	EKA	Cluster Platform 3000 BL 460c

World's
MOST-VISITED SHOPPING SITE

eBay

When online shoppers are looking to spend money, the majority check **EBAY** first. With 79.8 million visitors each month, eBay truly is the World's Online Marketplace®. The company was founded in 1995, and the online auction and shopping Web site attracts sellers and bidders from all over the world. Each year, millions of items—including spectacular treasures, unusual services, and even worthless junk—trade hands. Some of the most expensive sales include a Grumman Gulfstream II jet for $4.9 million and a 1909 Honus Wagner baseball card for $1.65 million.

WORLD'S MOST-VISITED SHOPPING SITES

Users who visited at least once during July 2007, in millions

eBay.com	Amazon.com	Apple.com	Target.com	Walmart.com
79.8	52.7	42.6	30.4	29.2

218

Country with the
HIGHEST INTERNET USE

Norway

About 88% of the NORWEGIAN POPULATION is surfing the Internet. That means about 4,074,000 people in the small European country have online access. And approximately 1.4 million of those people have broadband connections. Norway's Internet usage is also growing quickly—the percentage of users jumped 20% in just 2 years. The average Norwegian Web surfer spends about 25 hours online per week and views 2,913 pages.

COUNTRIES WITH THE HIGHEST INTERNET USE

Percentage of country

Norway	Netherlands	Iceland	Sweden	Portugal
88.0	87.8	85.4	77.3	73.1

Web sites, in millions

54.64	15.02	6.18	2.81	2.55
USA	Germany	UK	Canada	France

Country with the

MOST WEB SITES

COMPUTERS

United States

The UNITED STATES has the most sites on the World Wide Web with 54.6 million. That's more than half of the 100 million Web sites worldwide that make up the Internet today. There are currently more than 5,000 times more Web sites running today than were on the Web just 10 years ago. Web site production has increased at this incredible rate because sites have become so much easier to create. Bloggers and small business owners account for the largest percentage of new Web sites.

Country with the
MOST CELL PHONE ACCOUNTS

Italy

There are more than 123 cell phone accounts for every 100 people in ITALY. This means that some of the country's residents have 2 or more accounts. Cell phones are so popular in Italy because they are often cheaper than traditional land lines. The largest cell phone provider is Telcom Italia Mobil SpA with 25 million subscribers. The company introduced an extremely popular service that lets subscribers watch soccer video highlights on their phones and send clips and messages to friends. In the first month this service was available, more than 500,000 messages were sent.

220

COUNTRIES WITH THE MOST CELL PHONE ACCOUNTS

Cell phone accounts, per 100 people

Italy	Israel	Czech Republic	UK	Portugal
123.1	122.7	119.0	116.4	116.0

221

Country with the
MOST CELL PHONE SUBSCRIBERS

China

There are 461 million cell phone subscribers in CHINA, and that number is growing fast. Approximately 4 million people sign up for a new cell phone each month. Many Chinese people have at least 2 phones, using one for business and one for personal use. Not surprisingly, China is the main target market for new phones and technology. The country is also doing its part to recycle outdated phones—so far they have collected 3 tons of discarded handsets.

COUNTRIES WITH THE MOST CELL PHONE SUBSCRIBERS

Subscribers, in millions

China	USA	India	Russia	Japan
461.0	233.0	166.1	120.0	101.7

222

Country that watches the
MOST TV

United States

COUNTRIES THAT WATCH THE MOST TV

Each household in the UNITED STATES watches an average of 56.7 hours of TV per week. That's the equivalent of almost 123 straight days, or 4 months! The average adult watches about 4 hours per day, and the average child watches more than 3 hours. Some 98% of American households own at least 1 television, and about 54% of children have a set in their bedrooms. In 1 year, a child will see about 30,000 commercials. By age 65, a person will have watched more than 2 million television ads.

Average daily household TV viewing, in hours per week

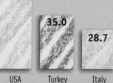

USA	Turkey	Italy	Belgium	Japan
56.7	35.0	28.7	27.0	25.9

Planet with the

MOST MOONS

Number of moons

Jupiter	Saturn	Uranus	Neptune	Mars
63	60	27	13	2

Jupiter

JUPITER—the fifth planet from the Sun—has 63 moons. Most of these moons—also called satellites—do not resemble traditional moons. Most are quite small, measuring from just 0.62 miles (0.99 km) to 4 miles (6.4 km) across. Jupiter's 4 largest moons are Ganymede, Europa, Io, and Callisto. The smaller moons travel in an elliptical, or egg-shaped, orbit in the opposite direction than Jupiter rotates. Astronomers believe these irregular moons formed somewhere else in the solar system and were pulled into orbit by Jupiter's gravity when they passed too close to the planet. Astronomers are constantly finding new moons for several of the planets, partly because of the highly sensitive telescopes and cameras now available to them.

223

Star that is
CLOSEST TO EARTH

Proxima Centauri

PROXIMA CENTAURI is approximately 24.7925 trillion miles (39.9233 trillion km) from Earth, making it our closest star other than the Sun. Light from the star reaches Earth in just 4.2 years. It is the third member of the Alpha Centauri triple system. This tiny red dwarf star is about 10% of the Sun's mass and .006% as bright. The surface temperature is thought to be about 3,000°F (1,650°C). More accurate measures of the star's size are not possible because it is so small. But these measurements are enough to cause scientists to believe that Proxima Centauri does not have any planets orbiting it that support life. If planets did exist, they would be too cold and dark for life-forms to exist.

224

STARS THAT ARE CLOSEST TO EARTH

Distance, in trillions of miles (kilometers)

Proxima Centauri	Alpha Centauri	Barnard's Star	Wolf 359	Lalande 21185
24.8 (39.9)	25.6 (41.2)	35.1 (56.6)	45.5 (73.3)	48.3 (77.8)

225

Planet with the
HOTTEST SURFACE

Venus

SOLAR SYSTEM'S HOTTEST PLANETS

The surface temperature on VENUS can reach a sizzling 870°F (465°C). That's approximately 19 times hotter than the average temperature on Earth. About every 19 months, Venus is closer to Earth than any other planet in the solar system. Venus is covered by a dense atmosphere. There are clouds made of acid, hurricane-strength winds, and lots of lightning. This makes it difficult to know what features are on its surface. The atmosphere also reflects a great deal of sunlight. At times, Venus is the third-brightest object in the sky, after the Sun and the Moon.

Average daytime temperature, in degrees Fahrenheit (Celsius)

Venus	Mercury	Earth	Mars	Jupiter
870 (465)	725 (385)	68 (20)	-76 (-60)	-160 (-107)

226

Planet with the
FASTEST ORBIT

Mercury

MERCURY orbits the Sun at about 30 miles (48 km) per second. At this astonishing speed, the planet can circle the Sun in about 88 Earth days. On Mercury, a solar day (the time from one sunrise to the next) lasts about 176 Earth days. Mercury's surface resembles that of Earth's moon, with flat plains, steep cliffs, and craters. Even though Mercury is the closest planet to the Sun, the temperature on the planet can change drastically. During the day, it can reach as high as 840°F (448°C), but at night, temperatures can fall to around -300°F (-184°C)!

PLANETS WITH THE FASTEST ORBITS

Orbital velocity, in miles (kilometers) per second

Mercury	Venus	Earth	Mars	Jupiter
29.75 (47.88)	21.76 (35.02)	18.51 (29.79)	14.51 (23.35)	8.12 (13.07)

THE SOLAR SYSTEM'S LARGEST PLANETS

Mean radius, in miles (kilometers)

43,411 (69,863)	36,184 (59,246)	15,759 (25,361)	15,301 (24,624)	3,959 (6,371)
Jupiter	Saturn	Uranus	Neptune	Earth

Solar System's

LARGEST PLANET

Jupiter

JUPITER has a radius of 43,441 miles (69,863 km)—that's almost 11 times larger than Earth's radius. In fact, Earth could fit inside Jupiter more than 1,000 times! Jupiter is about 480 million miles (772 million km) from the Sun. It takes almost 12 Earth years for Jupiter to make 1 complete orbit around the Sun. Although it is very large, Jupiter has a high rotation speed. One Jupiter day is less than 10 Earth hours long. That is the shortest solar day in the solar system.

227

228

Planet with the
MOST RINGS

Saturn

Scientists estimate that approximately 1,000 rings circle SATURN—hundreds more than any other planet. This ring system is only about 328 feet (100 m) thick, but reaches a diameter of 167,780 miles (270,015 km). The 3 major rings around the planet are named A, B, and C. Although they appear solid, Saturn's rings are made of particles of planet and satellite matter that range in size from about 1 to 15 feet (0.3 to 4.5 m). Because of the rings' brightness, scientists believe they are not as old as the planet they circle. Saturn, which is the sixth planet from the Sun, is the solar system's second-largest planet in size and mass.

PLANETS WITH THE MOST RINGS

Number of rings

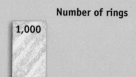

Saturn	Uranus	Neptune	Jupiter
1,000	11	6	1

Solar System's

LARGEST MOON

Ganymede

GANYMEDE is the largest moon of both Jupiter and the solar system. It has a diameter of 3,270 miles (5,262 km). That is almost 2.5 times larger than Earth's moon. The moon is approximately 1.4 million miles (2.25 million km) away from Jupiter and has an orbital period of about 7 days. It is probably made up mostly of rock and ice. It also has lava flows, mountains, and valleys. Many of the moon's large craters were caused by collisions with comets. Ganymede has both light and dark areas that give it a textured appearance. Ganymede was discovered by Galileo Galilei and Simon Marius almost 400 years ago.

229

SOLAR SYSTEM'S LARGEST MOONS

Diameter, in miles (kilometers)

3,270 (5,262)	3,200 (5,150)	2,995 (4,820)	2,264 (3,643)	2,160 (3,476)
Ganymede	Titan	Callisto	Io	Earth's moon

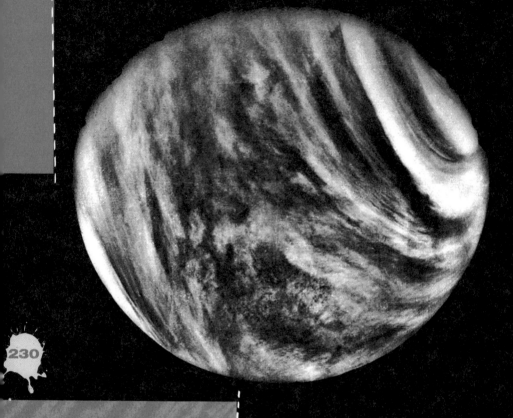

230

Solar System's
BRIGHTEST PLANET

Venus

VENUS is the brightest planet visible from Earth at night with a magnitude of -4.4. The planet can often be seen by the naked eye, or with a pair of binoculars. Venus appears so bright to sky gazers because it is the closest planet to Earth, and its thick clouds reflect the Sun's light. But because of this cloud cover, a simple telescope cannot reveal the planet's features. The geography of Venus consists mainly of huge plains, lowlands, and highlands.

SOLAR SYSTEM'S BRIGHTEST PLANETS

Apparent magnitude

Venus	Jupiter	Mars	Mercury	Saturn
-4.4	-2.7	-2.0	-1.9	0.7

Universe's
BRIGHTEST GALAXY

Large Magellanic Cloud

The **LARGE MAGELLANIC CLOUD** (LMC) is the brightest galaxy in the universe with an apparent magnitude of 0.91. First noted by the explorer Ferdinand Magellan in 1519, the LMC is a small galaxy in the southern constellations. Approximately 160,000 light-years from Earth, the LMC is an irregular dwarf galaxy that orbits the Milky Way. It is full of gas and dust, and new stars are continually forming within it. It is approximately one-twentieth the size of Earth's galaxy and contains about one-tenth the number of stars.

231

UNIVERSE'S BRIGHTEST GALAXIES

Apparent magnitude

Large Magellanic Cloud	Small Magellanic Cloud	Andromeda Galaxy	Triangulum Galaxy	Centaurus Galaxy
0.91	2.70	4.36	6.27	7.84

Planet with the

LONGEST DAY

Mercury

One day on MERCURY—from sunrise to sunset—lasts for 4,223.56 hours. That's equal to 176 Earth days! Mercury's unique orbit is responsible for the extra-long day.

Mercury is the fastest-moving planet, traveling around the Sun once every 88 Earth days. Mercury is the smallest planet in the solar system, and it is the closest one to the Sun. Because the planet is moving so quickly around the Sun, but spinning so slowly on its axis, it takes almost half an Earth year for a Mercury day to pass.

232

PLANETS WITH THE LONGEST DAYS

Length of day, in hours

4,223.56	2,802.00	24.03	24.00	17.01
Mercury	Venus	Mars	Earth	Uranus

233

World's
LONGEST SPACE WALK

Susan Helms & James Voss

THE WORLD'S LONGEST SPACE WALKS

SUSAN HELMS and JAMES VOSS each completed a space walk that lasted 8 hours and 56 minutes on March 11, 2001. The two astronauts spent the time working on the International Space Station. They prepped a shuttle docking tunnel which needed to be moved to make room for a cargo carrier. The astronauts also attached a mounting platform that would eventually support the station's robotic arm. And even though the space walk was the longest in NASA history, the astronauts did not have time for certain maintenance tasks, which were rescheduled for the future.

Length of space walk, in hours and minutes

8:56	8:56	8:29	8:29	8:29
James Voss	Susan Helms	Thomas Akers	Richard Hieb	Pierre Thuout

Stream of the
Canis Major galaxy

Sun

Canis Major
Galaxy

Milky Way

234

Galaxy

CLOSEST TO EARTH

Canis Major Dwarf

The CANIS MAJOR DWARF GALAXY is the Milky Way's closest neighbor, located just 42,000 light-years from Earth. The small galaxy was discovered by astronomers from France, Italy, the UK, and Australia in 2003. The astronomers used infrared light to see past the dust in the Milky Way. This study picked up the galaxy's cool, red stars that shine brightly in infrared light. Astronomers believe that the Canis Major Dwarf is gradually being ripped apart by the Milky Way's gravitational pull.

GALAXIES CLOSEST TO EARTH

Distance from Earth, in light-years

				205,000
			190,000	
		160,000		
	82,000			
42,000				
Canis Major Dwarf	Sagittarius Dwarf	Large Magellanic Cloud	Small Magellanic Cloud	Draco Dwarf

Sales, in millions of units in 2007

4.12	2.72	2.52	2.48	1.91
Wii Play with Remote (Wii)	Guitar Hero III: Legends of Rock (PS2)	Super Mario Galaxy (Wii)	Pokémon Diamond (DS)	Madden NFL 08 (PS2)

Wii Play with Remote

The WII PLAY WITH REMOTE sold a whopping 4.12 million games during 2007. That's enough copies to give one to every person living in the entire Dallas/Fort Worth, Texas area. The Wii Play with Remote features nine individual games, including *Billiards*, *Charge!*, *Fishing*, *Tanks*, *Find Mii*, *Laser Hockey*, *Table Tennis*, *Pose Mii*, and *Shooting Range*. Nintendo's Wii gaming console has been extremely popular since it went on sale in the fall of 2006—selling a unit every 17 seconds on Amazon.com during 2007.

235

World's
FASTEST PRODUCTION MOTORCYCLE

Suzuki GSX1300R Hayabusa

This sleek speed machine, which is named after one of the world's fastest birds, is able to reach a maximum speed of 186 miles (299 km) per hour. That's about 3 times faster than the speed limit on most major highways. The 2007 HAYABUSA features a 1299-cc, liquid-cooled DOHC engine. Its aerodynamic shape, 4-cylinder engine, and 6-speed transmission make the bike very popular with motorcycle enthusiasts. In 2001, motorcycle manufacturers set a guideline stating that no new production motorcycles will have a top speed above 186 miles (299 km) per hour, for safety reasons.

WORLD'S FASTEST PRODUCTION MOTORCYCLES

Maximum miles (kilometers) per hour

186 (299)	185 (297)	181 (291)	180 (289)	173 (278)
Suzuki GSX1300R Hayabusa	Kawasaki ZX-12R	Honda CBR1100XX	Harris Yamaha YLR500	Kawasaki ZZ-R1200

237

World's
FASTEST LAND VEHICLE

Thrust SSC

The THRUST SSC, which stands for Supersonic Car, reached a speed of 763 miles (1,228 km) per hour on October 15, 1997. At that speed, a car could make it from San Francisco to New York City in less than 4 hours. The Thrust SSC is propelled by 2 jet engines capable of 110,000 horsepower. It has the same power as 1,000 Ford Escorts or 145 Formula One race cars. The Thrust SSC runs on jet fuel, using about 5 gallons (19 L) per second. It only takes approximately 5 seconds for this supersonic car to reach its top speed. It is 54 feet (16.5 m) long and weighs 7 tons (6.4 t).

VEHICLES WITH THE FASTEST SPEEDS ON LAND

Speed, in miles (kilometers) per hour

763 (1,228)	633 (1,019)	622 (1,001)	600 (966)	576 (927)
Thrust SSC, 1997	Thrust 2, 1983	Blue Flame, 1970	Spirit of America, 1965	Green Monster, 1965

238

World's
FASTEST PASSENGER TRAIN

MagLev

The super speedy MAGLEV train in China carries passengers from Pudong financial district to Pudong International Airport at an average speed of 243 miles (391 km) per hour. The train reaches a top speed of 267 miles (430 km) per hour about 4 minutes into the trip. The 8-minute train ride replaces a 45-minute car trip. A one-way ticket costs about $6.50. The MagLev, which is short for magnet levitation, actually floats in the air just above the track. Tiny magnets are used to suspend the train, and larger ones are used to pull it forward. The German-built train began commercial operation in 2004.

WORLD'S FASTEST PASSENGER TRAINS

Average speed, in miles (kilometers) per hour

Train	Average speed
Maglev, China	243.0 (391.2)
Nozomi, Japan	162.6 (261.7)
TGV, France	158.0 (255.7)
Acela Express, USA	150.0 (241.0)
TGV Thalys, International	131.2 (211.1)

VEHICLES

World's
FASTEST PRODUCTION CAR

SSC Ultimate Aero

Maximum speed, in miles (kilometers) per hour

256 (412)	252 (406)	250 (402)	248 (399)	240 (386)
SSC Ultimate Aero	Bugatti Veyron	Koenig-segg CCX	Saleen S7 Twin Turbo	McLaren F1

The super speedy SSC ULTIMATE AERO can reach a top speed of 256 miles (412 km) per hour! At that rate, a person could drive from New York City to San Francisco in just 11.5 hours. The Aero can accelerate from 0 to 60 miles per hour in just 2.78 seconds, and cover a quarter mile in just 9.9 seconds. The Aero is powered by a twin turbo V-8 engine producing 1,183 horsepower. The SSC Ultimate Aero is built by Shelby Super Cars, and the design took 7 years to perfect.

239

World's
LARGEST CRUISE SHIP

Freedom of the Seas, Independence of the Seas, & Liberty of the Seas

Royal Caribbean's family of gigantic ships—*FREEDOM OF THE SEAS*, *INDEPENDENCE OF THE SEAS*, and *LIBERTY OF THE SEAS*—each weigh a whopping 160,000 tons (145,149 t) and measure 1,112 feet (339 m) long. Each of these luxury cruise liners offers vacationers some amazing ways to pass the day, including the FlowRider surfing pool, a full-sized ice skating rink, a rock-climbing wall, a mini golf course, and a sport court. The *Freedom of the Seas* was the first to set sail in June 2006, followed by the *Liberty of the Seas* in May 2007, and then the *Independence of the Seas* in May 2008.

WORLD'S LARGEST CRUISE SHIPS

Weight, in gross tons (tonnes)

Freedom of the Seas	Independence of the Seas	Liberty of the Seas	Queen Mary 2	Adventure of the Seas
160,000 (145,600)	160,000 (145,600)	160,000 (145,600)	151,400 (137,350)	138,000 (125,580)

World's
BIGGEST MONSTER TRUCK

Bigfoot 5

The BIGFOOT 5 truly is a monster—it measures 15.4 feet (4.7 m) high! That's about 3 times the height of an average car. Bigfoot 5 has 10-foot (3 m) Firestone Tundra tires, each weighing 2,400 pounds (1,088 kg), giving the truck a total weight of about 38,000 pounds (17,236 kg). The giant wheels were from an arctic snow train operated in Alaska by the US Army in the 1950s. This modified 1996 Ford F250 pickup truck is owned by Bob Chandler of St. Louis, Missouri. The great weight of this monster truck makes it too large to race.

WORLD'S BIGGEST MONSTER TRUCKS

Height, in feet (meters)

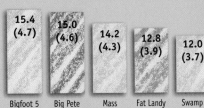

Bigfoot 5	Big Pete	Mass Destruction	Fat Landy	Swamp Thing
15.4 (4.7)	15.0 (4.6)	14.2 (4.3)	12.8 (3.9)	12.0 (3.7)

242

World's
LIGHTEST JET

BD-5J Microjet

The BD-5J MICROJET weighs only 358.8 pounds (162.7 kg), making it the lightest jet in the world. At only 12 feet (3.7 m) in length, it is one of the smallest as well. This tiny jet has a height of 5.6 feet (1.7 m) and a wingspan of 17 feet (5.2 m). The Microjet uses a TRS-18 turbojet engine. It can reach a top speed of 320 miles (514.9 km) per hour, but can only carry 32 gallons (121 L) of fuel at a time. A new BD-5J costs around $200,000. This high-tech gadget was flown by James Bond in the movie *Octopussy*, and it is also occasionally used by the U.S. military.

WORLD'S LIGHTEST JETS

Weight, in pounds (kilograms)

BD-5J Microjet	Cri-Cri Jet	Silver Bullet	SMART-1	McDonnell XF-85 Goblin
358.8 (162.7)	374.0 (169.6)	412.0 (186.9)	465.0 (210.9)	5,600 (2,540)

Speed, in miles (kilometers) per hour

7,459 (12,004)	2,436 (3,920)	2,193 (3,529)	2,154 (3,466)	1,903 (3,062)
X-43A	MiG-25R Foxbat-B	Lockheed SR-71 Blackbird	MiG-31 Foxhound	F-15 Eagle

World's
FASTEST PLANE

X-43A

NASA's experimental X-43A plane reached a top speed of Mach 9.8—or more than 9 times the speed of sound—on a test flight over the Pacific Ocean in November 2004. The X-43A was mounted on top of a Pegasus rocket booster and was carried into the sky by a B-52 aircraft. The booster was then fired, taking the X-43A about 110,000 feet (33,530 m) above the ground. The rocket was detached from the unmanned X-43A, and the plane flew unassisted for several minutes. At this rate of 7,459 miles (12,004 km) per hour, a plane could circle Earth in just over three and a half hours!

243

World's
FASTEST ROLLER COASTER
Kingda Ka

KINGDA KA—the newest coaster at Six Flags Great Adventure in Jackson, New Jersey—can launch riders straight up a track at a top speed of 128 miles (206 km) per hour. This hydraulic launch coaster reaches its top speed in less than 4 seconds. Kingda Ka is also the world's tallest rollercoaster at 456 feet (139 m). In addition to the horizontal rocket that starts the ride, the coaster also features a few breathtaking drops and spiral turns. The 50-second-long ride cost $25 million to build and debuted during the 2005 season.

244

WORLD'S FASTEST ROLLERCOASTERS

Speed, in miles (kilometers) per hour

128 (206)	120 (193)	106 (172)	100 (161)	100 (161)
Kingda Ka, USA	Top Thrill Dragster, USA	Dodonpa, Japan	Superman The Escape, USA	Tower of Terror, Australia

US Records

Alabama to Wyoming

246

State with the
OLDEST MARDI GRAS

Alabama

People in Mobile, ALABAMA, have been celebrating Mardi Gras since 1703, but did not have an official parade event until 1831. After a brief hiatus during the Civil War, the celebrations started back up in 1866 and have been growing ever since. Today, some 100,000 people gather in Mobile to enjoy the 22 parades that take place during the two weeks that lead up to Mardi Gras. On the biggest day—Fat Tuesday—six parades wind through the downtown waterfront, with floats and costumed dancers. But at the stroke of midnight, the partying stops and plans for next year begin.

UNITED STATES' OLDEST MARDI GRAS CELEBRATIONS

Number of years since celebration began*

Mobile, Alabama 1831	New Orleans, Louisiana 1835	Lafayette, Louisiana 1842	Pensacola, Florida 1844	Galveston, Texas 1867
177	173	166	164	141

*As of 2008

State with the

LARGEST NATIONAL FOREST

Alaska

The Tongass National Forest covers approximately 26,250 square miles (67,987 sq km) in southeast ALASKA. That's about the same size as West Virginia. It is also home to the world's largest temperate rain forest. Some of the forest's trees are more than 700 years old. About 11,000 miles (17,703 km) of shoreline are inside the park. Some of the animals that live in the forest include bears, salmon, and wolves. The world's largest concentration of bald eagles also spend the fall and winter here on the Chilkat River.

247

UNITED STATES' LARGEST NATIONAL FORESTS

Size, in square miles (square kilometers)

26,250 (67,987)	8,433 (21,841)	5,051 (13,082)	4,489 (11,626)	4,232 (10,960)
Tongass National Forest, Alaska	Chugach National Forest, Alaska	Toiyabe National Forest, Nevada	Tonto National Forest, Arizona	Gila National Forest, New Mexico

State with the
SUNNIEST PLACE

Arizona

The little town of Yuma, ARIZONA, enjoys bright, sunny days approximately 90% of the year. That means that the sun is shining about 328 days out of each year! Yuma is located in southwestern Arizona near the borders of California and Mexico. Although the temperatures are normally in the 70s year-round, the dry desert air keeps the humidity low. And this sunny spot is drawing a crowd—Yuma is the third-fastest growing area in the United States.

SOME OF THE UNITED STATES' SUNNIEST PLACES

Percentage of sunny days per year

Yuma, Arizona	Redding, California	Scottsdale, Arizona	Las Vegas, Nevada	El Paso, Texas
90	88	86	85	84

248

249

State with the
LARGEST RETAIL HEAD-QUARTERS

Arkansas

Wal-Mart—headquartered in Bentonville, ARKANSAS—logged $345 billion in sales in 2007. The company was founded in 1962 by Arkansas native Sam Walton, who saw his small variety stores grow into giant grocery stores, membership warehouse clubs, and deep-discount warehouse outlets. Walton's original store in Bentonville now serves as the company's visitor center. Each year, the company gives back some of what it earns to more than 100,000 charitable and community-based organizations.

UNITED STATES' LARGEST RETAIL HEADQUARTERS

2007 sales, in billions of US dollars

$345.0				
	$90.8	$66.1	$64.4	$63.4
Wal-Mart, Arkansas	The Home Depot, Georgia	Kroger, Ohio	Costco, Washington	Target, Minnesota

250

State with the

HIGHEST AVOCADO PRODUCTION

California

CALIFORNIA is the country's top producer of avocados—harvesting about 259 tons (235.2 t), or 96% of the United States' crop. California has about 65,000 acres (26,305 ha) of avocado trees, and together they produce a crop worth $244.9 million. In one year, a single avocado tree can produce some 60 pounds (27.2 kg), or about 150 pieces, of fruit. Because of its warm coastal climate, the state can grow avocados year-round. The town of Fallbrook is known as the Avocado Capital of the World and hosts the annual Avocado Festival.

UNITED STATES' TOP AVOCADO PRODUCERS

Production, in tons (metric tons)

California	Florida	Hawaii
259.3 (235.2)	6.0 (5.4)	0.8 (0.73)

BASEROLL TEAMS WITH THE HIGHEST SEASONAL ATTENDANCE

Seasonal attendance, in millions

4.48	4.27	3.77	3.60	3.48
Colorado Rockies, 1993	New York Yankees, 2007	New York Yankees, 2004	Los Angeles Dodgers, 2005	Los Angeles Dodgers, 2004

State's Baseball Team with the

HIGHEST SEASONAL ATTENDANCE

Colorado

In 1993, the seasonal attendance for the COLORADO Rockies was an impressive 4.48 million fans. The Rockies finished up their inaugural season in October of the same year with the most wins by a National League expansion team. The Rockies played at Mile High Stadium for their first two years. The team moved to Denver's Coors Field in 1995. The new park was designed to have 43,800 seats, but with such high attendance at Mile High Stadium, architects reworked the plans to include 50,200 seats. The team proceeded to sell out 203 consecutive games.

251

State with the
OLDEST THEME PARK

Connecticut

Lake Compounce in Bristol, CONNECTICUT, first opened as a picnic park in 1846. The park's first electric roller coaster, the Green Dragon, was introduced in 1914 and cost 10 cents per ride. It was replaced by the WildCat in 1927, and the wooden coaster still operates today. In 1996 the park got a $50 million upgrade, which included the thrilling new roller coaster Boulder Dash. It is the only coaster to be built into a mountainside. Another $3.3 million was spent on upgrades in 2005, including an 800-foot (244-m) lazy river.

UNITED STATES' OLDEST THEME PARKS

Number of years open*

162	138	130	129	114
Lake Compounce, Connecticut 1846	Cedar Point, Ohio 1870	Idlewild Park, Pennsylvania 1878	Seabreeze Park, New York 1879	Lakemont Park, Pennsylvani 1894

*As of 2008

252

253

LARGEST PUMPKIN-THROWING CONTEST

Delaware

Each year approximately 28,000 people gather in Sussex County, DELAWARE, for the annual World Championship Punkin Chunkin. More than 60 teams compete during the three-day festival to see who can chuck their pumpkin the farthest. Each team constructs a machine that has a mechanical or compressed-air firing device—no explosives are allowed. The farthest a pumpkin has traveled during the championship is 4,434 feet (1,352 m), or the length of twelve football fields. The total combined distance of all the pumpkins chunked at the 2007 championship totaled almost 12 miles (19 km). Each year the festival raises about $100,000 and benefits St. Jude Children's Hospital.

UNITED STATES' LARGEST PUMPKIN-THROWING CONTESTS

Spectators

Location	Spectators
Millsboro, Delaware	28,000
Morton, Illinois	4,000
York, Pennsylvania	3,000
Busti, New York	2,500
Salina, Kansas	1,500

State with the

MOST LIGHTNING STRIKES

Florida

Southern FLORIDA is known as the Lightning Capital of the United States, with 25.1 bolts occurring over each square mile (2.6 sq km)—the equivalent of 10 city blocks—each year. Some 70% of all strikes occur between noon and 6:00 P.M., and the most dangerous months are July and August. Most lightning bolts measure 2 to 3 miles (5.2 to 7.8 km) long and can generate between 100 million and 1 billion volts of electricity. The air in a lightning bolt is heated to 50,000° F (27,760° C).

STATES WITH THE MOST LIGHTNING STRIKES

Annual bolts per square mile (2.6 sq km)

Florida	Louisiana	Mississippi	Texas	Arizona
25.1	17.1	15.5	15.0	13.9

255

State with the
LARGEST SPORTS HALL OF FAME

Georgia

The GEORGIA Sports Hall of Fame fills 43,000 square feet (3,995 sq m) with memorabilia from Georgia's most accomplished prep, college, amateur, and professional athletes. Some 230,000 bricks, 245 tons (222 t) of steel, and 7,591 pounds (3,443 kg) of glass were used in its construction. The hall owns more than 3,000 artifacts and displays about 1,000 of them at a time. Some Hall of Famers include baseball legend Hank Aaron, Olympic basketball great Theresa Edwards, and Super Bowl I champion Bill Curry.

STATES WITH THE LARGEST SPORTS HALLS OF FAME

Area, in square feet (square meters)

43,000 (3,995)	33,000 (3,066)	32,000 (3,000)	21,542 (2,001)	20,000 (1,900)
Georgia Sports Hall of Fame	Alabama Sports Hall of Fame	Virgina Sports Hall of Fame	Mississippi Sports Hall of Fame	Kansas Sports Hall of Fame

256

State with the

LARGEST SUBMILLIMETER WAVELENGTH TELESCOPE

Mauna Kea—located on the island of HAWAII—is the home to the world's largest submillimeter wavelength telescope, with a diameter of 49 feet (15 m). The James Clerk Maxwell Telescope (JCMT) is used to study our solar system, interstellar dust and gas, and distant galaxies. Mauna Kea also houses the world's largest optical/infrared (Keck I and II) and dedicated infrared (UKIRT) telescopes in the world. Mauna Kea is an ideal spot for astronomy because the atmosphere above the dormant volcano is very dry with little cloud cover, and its distance from city lights ensures a dark night sky.

Hawaii

WORLD'S LARGEST SUBMILLIMETER WAVELENGTH TELESCOPES

Diameter of lens, in feet (meters)

49 (15)	34.0 (10.4)	32.8 (10)	32.8 (10)	32.8 (10)
James Clerk Maxwell Telescope (JCMT), Hawaii	Caltech Submillimeter Observatory (CSO), Hawaii	Atacama Submillimeter Telescope (ASTE), Chile	Heinrich Hertz Telescope (HHT), Arizona	Submillimeter Telescope (SMT), Arizona

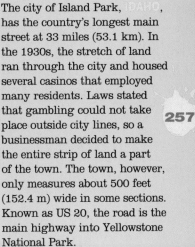

State with the

LONGEST MAIN STREET

Idaho

The city of Island Park, IDAHO, has the country's longest main street at 33 miles (53.1 km). In the 1930s, the stretch of land ran through the city and housed several casinos that employed many residents. Laws stated that gambling could not take place outside city lines, so a businessman decided to make the entire strip of land a part of the town. The town, however, only measures about 500 feet (152.4 m) wide in some sections. Known as US 20, the road is the main highway into Yellowstone National Park.

257

UNITED STATES' LONGEST MAIN STREETS

Length, in miles (kilometers)

33 (53.1)	29 (46.7)	13 (20.9)	10 (16.1)	9.2 (14.8)
US Highway 20, Island Park, Idaho	Main Street, Houston, Texas	US Highway 35, Maiden Rock, Wisconsin	US Highway 83, Cordon, Montana	Main Street, Belleville, Illinois

State with the

LARGEST COOKIE FACTORY

Illinois

The Nabisco factory covers 46 acres (18.6 ha) on South Kedzie Avenue in Chicago, ILLINOIS. The 1.75 million-square-foot (162,000-sq-m) cookie factory is also one of the largest bakeries in the world. The Nabisco plant employs about 2,000 workers, and they produce about 320 million pounds (145 million kg) of Oreo cookies, Fig Newtons, and Ritz Crackers each year. The factory has storage capacity for 8.5 million pounds (3.9 million kg) of flour, 2.4 million pounds (1.1 million kg) of sugar, and 1.5 million pounds (680,388 kg) of vegetable oil. There are also 20 ovens in the facility that measure about 300 feet (91 m) in length.

UNITED STATES' LARGEST COOKIE FACTORIES

Area, in square feet (square meters)

1.75 M (162,000)	500,000 (46,452)	325,000 (30,194)	265,000 (24,619)	97,000 (9,012)
Nabisco, Illinois	Entenmann's, New York	Interstate Bakeries Corporation, Missouri	Pepperidge Farm, Connecticut	Otis Spunkmeyer, Texas

State with the
LARGEST HALF MARATHON

Indiana

Cars aren't the only things racing in Indianapolis, INDIANA. Each May some 35,000 runners take part in the Indianapolis Life 500 Festival Mini-Marathon. This makes the mini-marathon the nation's largest half marathon and the nation's eighth longest road race. The 13.1-mile (21.1-km) race winds through downtown and includes a lap along the Indianapolis Motor Speedway oval. About 100 musical groups entertain the runners as they complete the course. A giant pasta dinner and after-race party await the runners at the end of the day. The mini-marathon is part of a weekend celebration that centers around the Indianapolis 500 auto race.

UNITED STATES' LARGEST HALF MARATHONS

Number of runners

Indianapolis Life 500 Festival Mini-Marathon, Indiana	County Race for the Cure, Michigan	Rock 'n' Roll Half Marathon, Arizona	Rock 'n' Roll Half Marathon, Virginia	Chicago Half Marathon, Illinois
35,000	25,000	24,000	20,000	18,000

State with the
HIGHEST EGG PRODUCTION

Iowa

IOWA tops all other states in the country in egg production, turning out approximately 13.9 billion eggs per year. That's enough to give every person in the United States about 3 and a half dozen eggs each! That's a good thing, because each person in America eats about 256 eggs per year. The state has 55 million laying hens, and each is capable of laying about 240 eggs a year. These hungry hens eat about 55 million bushels of corn and 27.5 million bushels of soybeans annually. In addition to selling the eggs as is, Iowa's processing plants turn them into frozen, liquid, dried, or specialty egg products.

260

UNITED STATES' TOP EGG PRODUCERS

Number of eggs produced annually, in billions

Iowa	Ohio	Indiana	Pennsylvania	Texas
13.87	7.15	6.67	6.39	4.99

261

State with the
WINDIEST CITY

Kansas

According to average annual wind speeds collected by the National Climatic Data Center, Dodge City, KANSAS is the windiest city in the United States, with an average wind speed of 14 miles (22.5 km) per hour. Located in Ford County, the city borders the Santa Fe Trail and is rich in history. The city was established in 1872 and had a reputation as a tough cowboy town. With help from legendary sheriffs like Wyatt Earp, order was restored and the town grew steadily. Today tourists come to take in the area history.

UNITED STATES' WINDIEST CITIES

Average wind speed, in miles (kilometers) per hour

Dodge City, Kansas	Amarillo, Texas	Rochester, Minnesota	Lihue, Hawaii	Chester, Minnesota
13.9 (22.4)	13.5 (21.7)	13.1 (21.1)	12.0 (20.8)	12.8 (20.6)

262

State with the

LARGEST FIREWORKS DISPLAY

Kentucky

Thunder Over Louisville is the world's largest fireworks display, drawing approximately 800,000 spectators each year. It is the opening ceremony for the KENTUCKY Derby Festival. Eight 400-foot (122-m) barges line both sides of the Second Street Bridge and serve as a stage for the 26-minute show. During the show, some 60 tons (54 t) of fireworks shells and 250 tons (227 t) of launching tubes are used. The show is set to all types of music, ranging from rock and roll to Broadway tunes. Millions of people worldwide also see the show when it's rebroadcast on the 4th of July to 150 countries.

UNITED STATES' LARGEST FIREWORKS DISPLAYS

Number of fireworks shells used

Thunder Over Louisville, Kentucky	Macy's 4th of July, New York	Sailfest, Connecticut	Pops Concert at the Esplanade, Massachusetts	Central Pennsylvania 4th Fest, Pennsylvania
60,000	40,000	22,900	12,000	10,500

Total number of alligators

Louisiana	Florida	Texas	Georgia	South Carolina
1.5 M	1.3 M	400,000	200,000	100,000

State with the
LARGEST ALLIGATOR POPULATION

Louisiana

There are approximately 1.5 million alligators living in LOUISIANA. About 1 million alligators live in the wild, and another half million are raised in farms. In 1986, Louisiana began an alligator ranching business, which encouraged farmers to raise thousands of the reptiles each year. The farmers must return some alligators to the wild, but they are allowed to sell the rest for profit. And, the released alligators have an excellent chance of thriving in the wild because they have been well fed and are a good size. Although alligators can be found in the state's bayous, swamps, and ponds, most live in Louisiana's 3 million acres (1.2 million ha) of coastal marshland.

GATOR XING
NEXT 1/2 MILE

263

264

State with the
OLDEST STATE FAIR

Maine

The first Skowhegan State Fair took place in 1819—a year before MAINE officially became a state! The fair took place in January, and hundreds of people came despite the harsh weather. Originally sponsored by the Somerset Central Agricultural Society, the fair name became official in 1842. State fairs were very important in the early 1900s. With no agricultural colleges in existence, fairs became the best way for farmers to learn about new agricultural methods and equipment. Today the Skowhegan State Fair features more than 7,000 exhibitors who compete for prize money totaling more than $200,000. The fair also includes a demolition derby, a children's barnyard, concerts, livestock exhibits, and arts and crafts.

UNITED STATES' OLDEST STATE FAIRS

Number of years since fair first held*

189	188	157	157	146
Skowhegan State Fair, Maine 1819	Three County Fair, Massachusetts 1820	Bangor State Fair, Maine 1851	Brooklyn Fair, Connecticut 1851	Woodstock Fair, Vermont 1862

*As of 2008

State with the
OLDEST AIRPORT

Maryland

The Wright brothers founded College Park Airport in 1909 to teach Army officers how to fly, and it has been in operation ever since. The airport is now owned by the MARYLAND-National Capital Park and Planning Commission and is on the Register of Historic Places. Many aviation "firsts" occurred at this airport, such as the first woman passenger in the United States (1909), the first test of a bomb-dropping device (1911), and the first US Air Mail Service (1918). The College Park Aviation Museum is located on the grounds and houses aviation memorabilia.

UNITED STATES' OLDEST AIRPORTS

Number of years open*

College Park Airport, Maryland 1909	Robertson Airport, Connecticut 1911	Hartness State Airport, Vermont 1920	Middlesboro-Bell County Airport, Kentucky 1921	Page Field, Florida 1924
99	97	88	87	84

*As of 2008

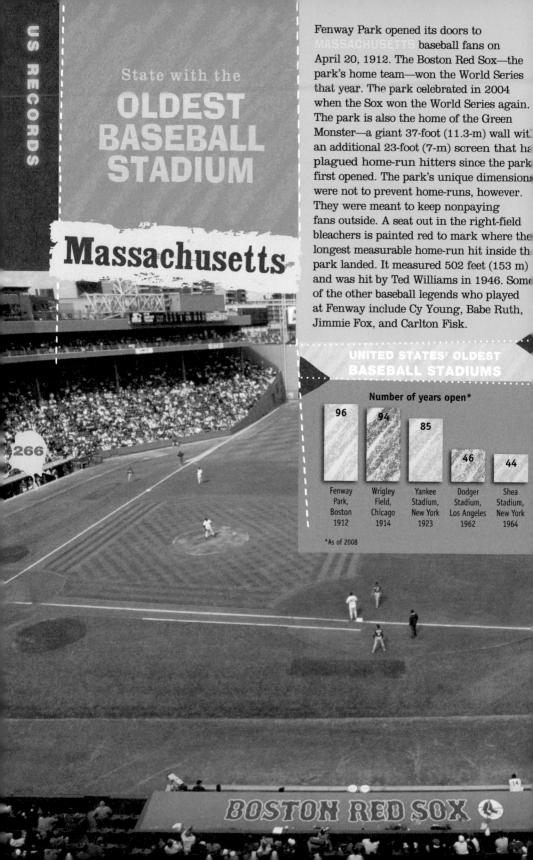

State with the

OLDEST BASEBALL STADIUM

Massachusetts

Fenway Park opened its doors to MASSACHUSETTS baseball fans on April 20, 1912. The Boston Red Sox—the park's home team—won the World Series that year. The park celebrated in 2004 when the Sox won the World Series again. The park is also the home of the Green Monster—a giant 37-foot (11.3-m) wall with an additional 23-foot (7-m) screen that has plagued home-run hitters since the park first opened. The park's unique dimensions were not to prevent home-runs, however. They were meant to keep nonpaying fans outside. A seat out in the right-field bleachers is painted red to mark where the longest measurable home-run hit inside the park landed. It measured 502 feet (153 m) and was hit by Ted Williams in 1946. Some of the other baseball legends who played at Fenway include Cy Young, Babe Ruth, Jimmie Fox, and Carlton Fisk.

UNITED STATES' OLDEST BASEBALL STADIUMS

Number of years open*

96	94	85	46	44
Fenway Park, Boston 1912	Wrigley Field, Chicago 1914	Yankee Stadium, New York 1923	Dodger Stadium, Los Angeles 1962	Shea Stadium, New York 1964

*As of 2008

266

BOSTON RED SOX

267

State with the

LARGEST INDOOR WATERFALL

Michigan

The 114-foot (34.7-m) waterfall located in the lobby of the International Center in Detroit, MICHIGAN, is the tallest indoor waterfall in the world. The backdrop of this impressive waterfall is a 9,000-square-foot (840-sq-m) slab of marble that was imported from the Greek island of Tinos and installed by eight marble craftsmen. About 6,000 gallons (27,276 L) of water spill down the waterfall each minute. That's the liquid equivalent of 80,000 cans of soda! Visitors can see this $1.5 million creation as they stroll through the International Center, which also houses many retail shops. Located in the historic Trappers Alley in the Greektown section of the city, the 8-story building was formerly used as a seed warehouse.

WORLD'S LARGEST INDOOR WATERFALLS

Height, in feet (meters)

International Center, Michigan	Trump Tower, New York	Orchid Hotel, India	Casino Windsor, Michigan	Mohegan Sun, Connecticut
114 (34.7)	90 (27.4)	70 (21.3)	60 (18.3)	55 (16.8)

State with the LARGEST INDOOR THEME PARK

Minnesota

The Park at MOA is located inside of the Mall of America in Bloomington, MINNESOTA, and covers 7 acres (2.8 ha). The park offers 30 rides, including the Xcel Energy Log Chute, skyscraper Ferris wheel, Timber Twister roller coaster, Mighty Axe, and the Mystery Mine Ride. Some of the other attractions at the park are a rock-climbing wall, petting zoo, and game arcade. In 2008, Nickelodeon Universe opened inside the Park, offering rides for kids and teens, games, and a food court. Kids can also meet Dora, Diego, Blue, and SpongeBob.

UNITED STATES' LARGEST INDOOR THEME PARKS

Area, in acres (hectares)

7 (2.8)	5 (2.0)	2.3 (0.9)	1.1 (0.45)	1 (0.40)
The Park at MOA, Minnesota	Adventure-dome Theme Park, Nevada	Disney-Quest, Florida	Great Wolf Lodge, Kansas	The Parthenon at Mt. Olympus, Wisconsin

269

State with the
MOST CATFISH

Mississippi

There are more than 530 million catfish in MISSISSIPPI—more than 55% of the world's farm-raised supply. That's almost enough to give every person in the state 235 fish each. Mississippi's catfish crop is worth about $218 million annually. There are about 360 catfish producers farming 100,000 water acres (40,468 ha). The state's residents are quite proud of their successful fish industry and celebrate at the World Catfish Festival in Belzoni.

STATES WITH THE MOST CATFISH

Number of catfish, in millions

Mississippi	Louisiana	Alabama	Arkansas	Texas
530	210	190	125	70

270

State with the

LARGEST OUTDOOR THEATER

Missouri

The Municipal Theatre in St. Louis, MISSOURI—affectionately known as The Muny—is the nation's largest outdoor theater, with 80,000 square feet (7,432 sq m) and 11,500 seats—about the same size as a regulation soccer field. Amazingly, construction on the giant theater was completed in just 42 days at a cost of $10,000. The theater opened in 1917 with a production of Verdi's *Aida*, and the best seats cost only $1.00. Today, The Muny offers classic Broadway shows each summer, with past productions including *Aida*, *The King and I*, *The Wizard of Oz*, and *Oliver!* And the last nine rows of the theater are always held as free seats for the public, just as they have been since The Muny opened.

UNITED STATES' LARGEST OUTDOOR THEATERS

Area, in square feet (square meters)

80,000 (7,432)	55,000 (5,100)	45,000 (4,200)	37,000 (3,500)	12,000 (1,100)
The Muny, Missouri	Alpine Valley Music Theater, Wisconsin	Journal Pavilion, New Mexico	Miller Outdoor Theater, Texas	Starlight Theater, Missouri

STATES WITH THE LARGEST BIGHORN SHEEP POPULATIONS

Number of sheep

6,100	5,200	4,300	2,250	495
Montana	Nevada	California	Utah	Colorado

State with the
LARGEST BIGHORN SHEEP POPULATION

Montana

With a population of 6,100 bighorn sheep, MONTANA has more of these wild endangered mammals than any other state. The population has quadrupled in the last 60 years. Many of Montana's bighorn sheep live in an area known as the Rocky Mountain Front—a 100-mile (160.9-km) area that stretches from Glacier National Park to the town of Lincoln. A ram's horns can weigh up to 30 pounds (13.6 kg)—more than all of the bones in its body. Rams use these giant horns when they butt heads with a rival sheep, and can hit each other at up to 20 miles (32.2 km) per hour.

271

272

LARGEST NOCTURNAL ANIMAL EXHIBIT

The Henry Doorly Zoo in Omaha, NEBRASKA, is home to the Kingdom of the Night exhibit, which occupies more than 42,000 square feet (3,901 sq m) of the zoo's Desert Dome. There are five different areas inside the 0.75 acre (0.3 ha) exhibit, including the canyon, the African diorama, the wet cave, the Eucalyptus forest, and the dry cave. The exhibit also houses the world's largest indoor swamp. The swamp has 160,000 gallons (605,666 L) of water and 30 different animal species. The zoo has reversed the daily cycle of these animals, making the exhibit light in the night and dark in the day, so the animals are most active when visitors are there.

Nebraska

UNITED STATES' LARGEST NOCTURNAL ANIMAL EXHIBITS

Area, in square feet (square meters)

Kingdoms of the Night, Nebraska	Animals of the Night, Tennessee	Day and Night Exhibit, Washington	Masters of the Night, Texas	Frogtown USA, Ohio
42,000 (3,901)	35,000 (3,252)	20,000 (1,858)	5,000 (465)	600 (56)

State with the

LARGEST GLASS SCULPTURE

Nevada

Fiori di Como—the breathtaking chandelier at the Bellagio Hotel in Las Vegas, NEVADA—measures 65.7 feet by 29.5 feet (20 m by 9 m). Created by Dale Chihuly, the handblown glass chandelier consists of more than 2,000 discs of colored glass. Each disc is about 18 inches (45.7 cm) wide and hangs about 20 feet (6.1 m) overhead. Together, these colorful discs look like a giant field of flowers. The chandelier required about 10,000 pounds (4,536 kg) of steel and 40,000 pounds (18,144 kg) of handblown glass. The sculpture's name translates to "Flowers of Como." The Bellagio was modeled after the hotel on Lake Como in Italy.

273

UNITED STATES' LARGEST GLASS SCULPTURES

Length, in feet (meters)

65.7 (20)	55 (16.8)	49.2 (15)	43 (13.1)	29 (8.8)
Fiori di Como, Nevada	The Chihuly Tower, Oklahoma	Borealis, Michigan	Fireworks of Glass, Indiana	Cobalt Blue Chandelier, Washington

State with the

OLDEST POST OFFICE

New Hampshire

The Hinsdale Post Office in NEW HAMPSHIRE opened its doors in 1816, and has been in operation ever since. At that time, James Madison was the country's fourth president and the Civil War was still 45 years away. The mail was delivered by horse and wagon and there were no paved roads. In the mid 1800s, nearby Brattleboro, Vermont, was connected to the railroad and mail was moved that way. In 1905, the first rural route was in place and mail was delivered to some homes by horse and buggy. Today the historic building is equipped with modern technology, and the price of a stamp is 3,100% higher than it was in 1816.

UNITED STATES' OLDEST POST OFFICES

Number of years open*

192	144	121	116	115
Hinsdale, New Hampshire 1816	Galena, Illinois 1859	Memphis, Tennessee 1887	Brooklyn, New York 1892	Hoboken, New Jersey 1893

*As of 2008

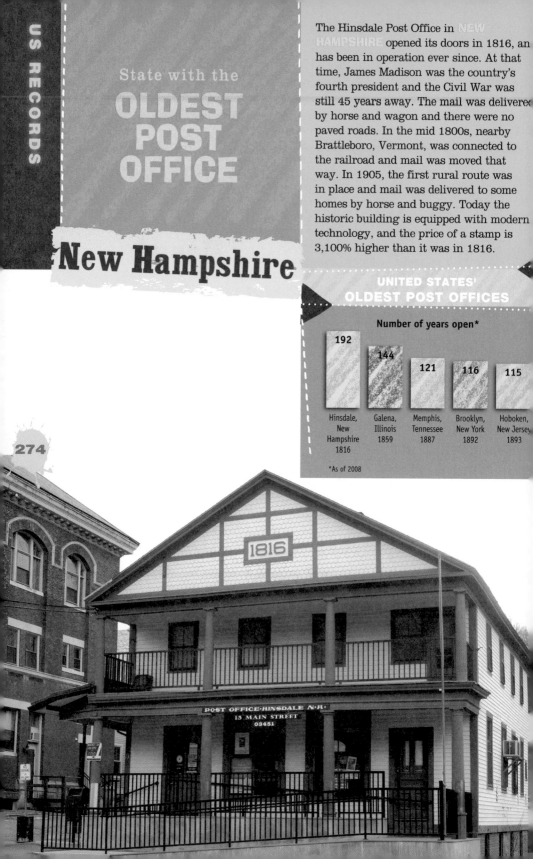

1816

POST OFFICE · HINSDALE N.H.
15 MAIN STREET
03451

275

State with the
LONGEST BOARDWALK

New Jersey

The famous boardwalk in Atlantic City, NEW JERSEY, stretches for 4 miles (6.4 km) along the beach. Combined with the adjoining boardwalk in Ventnor, the length increases to just under 6 miles (9.7 km). The 60-foot- (18-m) wide boardwalk opened on June 26, 1870. It was the first boardwalk built in the United States, and was designed to keep sand out of the tourists' shoes. Today the boardwalk is filled with amusement parks, shops, restaurants, and hotels. The boardwalk recently recieved a $100 million face-lift, which included new roofs, signs, and storefronts to surrounding buildings. About 37 million people take a stroll along the walk each year.

WORLD'S LONGEST BOARDWALKS

Length, in miles (kilometers)

4.0 (6.4)
Atlantic City, New Jersey

3.0 (4.8)
Coney Island, New York

2.5 (4.0)
FDR Boardwalk, New York

2.3 (3.7)
Corkscrew Swamp Sanctuary, Florida

2.0 (3.2)
Jarzoo Boardwalk, Sweden

State with the
LARGEST BALLOON FESTIVAL

New Mexico

During the 2007 Kodak Albuquerque International Balloon Fiesta in NEW MEXICO, approximately 700 hot air and gas-filled balloons sailed across the sky. Held each October, the Fiesta draws hundreds of thousands of spectators. This event attracts balloons from around the world, and is often seen in more than 50 countries. The festival takes place in the 365-acre (148-ha) Balloon Fiesta State Park. The Balloon Fiesta has also hosted some prestigious balloon races, including the Gordon Bennett Cup (1993), World Gas Balloon Championship (1994), and the America's Challenge Gas Balloon Race (2006).

276

WORLD'S LARGEST BALLOON FESTIVALS

Approximate number of balloons

700	200	150	150	100
Albuquerque, New Mexico	Gallup, New Mexico	Greenville, South Carolina	Gatineau, Canada	Colorado Springs, Colorado

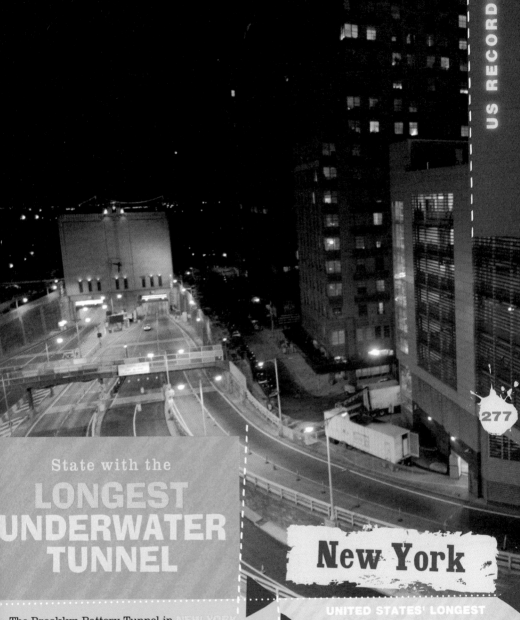

277

State with the
LONGEST UNDERWATER TUNNEL

New York

The Brooklyn-Battery Tunnel in NEW YORK measures 1.73 miles (2.78 km) long, making it the longest underwater tunnel in North America and longest continuous underwater vehicular tunnel in the world. The tunnel passes under the East River and connects Battery Park in Manhattan with the Red Hook section of Brooklyn. It took 13,900 tons (12,609 t) of steel, about 205,000 cubic yards (156,700 cu m) of concrete, approximately 1,871 miles (3,011 km) of electrical wire, some 883,391 bolts, and 799,000 wall and ceiling tiles to build the tunnel. Completed in 1950, the $90-million tunnel carries about 60,000 vehicles a day.

UNITED STATES' LONGEST UNDERWATER TUNNELS

Length, in miles (kilometers)

1.73 (2.78)	1.62 (2.62)	1.60 (2.57)	1.56 (2.51)	1.09 (1.75)
Brooklyn-Battery Tunnel, New York	Holland Tunnel, New York	Ted Williams Tunnel, Massachusetts	Lincoln Tunnel, New York	Thimble Shoal Tunnel, Viginia

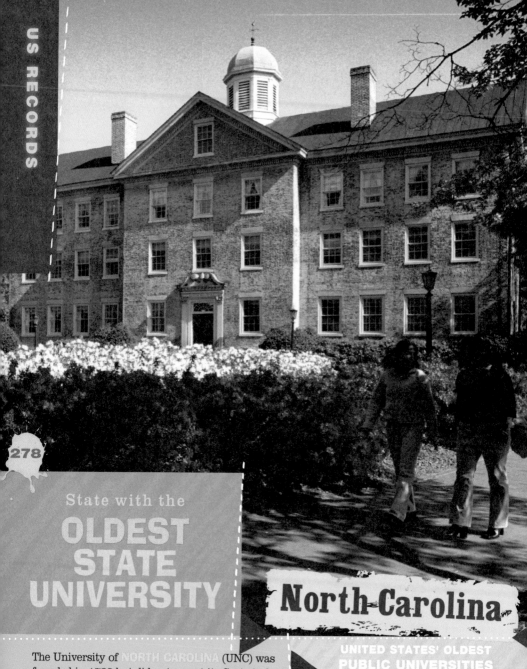

278

State with the

OLDEST STATE UNIVERSITY

North Carolina

The University of NORTH CAROLINA (UNC) was founded in 1789 but did not accept its first student at Chapel Hill until February 1795 because of a lack of funding. By the following month, the university consisted of two buildings, two professors, and 41 students. This makes UNC the only public university in the United States to graduate students in the 18th century. Today, the University of North Carolina's 16 campuses have more than 27,500 undergraduates and 3,100 faculty. The university offers more than 100 fields of study, and grants bachelor's, master's, and doctoral degrees.

UNITED STATES' OLDEST PUBLIC UNIVERSITIES

Number of years open*

213	207	205	205	180
University of North Carolina 1795	University of Vermont 1801	University of Georgia 1803	University of South Carolina 1803	State University of New York, New Paltz 1828

*As of 2008

UNITED STATES' TALLEST METAL SCULPTURES

Height, in feet (meters)

110 (33.5)
Geese in Flight, North Dakota

70 (21.3)
Bass Fish, North Dakota

70 (21.3)
Deer Crossing, North Dakota

60 (18.3)
Egyptian Longhorn, South Dakota

60 (18.3)
Needle Tower, Oregon

State with the
TALLEST METAL SCULPTURE

North Dakota

In August 2001, Gary Greff created a 110-foot- (33.5-m-) tall metal sculpture along the stretch of road between Gladstone and Regent, NORTH DAKOTA. That's the height of an 11-story building! The 154-foot- (46.9-m-) long sculpture is called *Geese in Flight,* and shows Canadian geese traveling across the prairie. Greff has created several other towering sculptures nearby, and the road has become known as the Enchanted Highway. He created these sculptures to attract tourists to the area and to support his hometown. He relies only on donations to finance his work.

279

State with the

LARGEST TWINS GATHERING

Ohio

Each August, the town of Twinsburg, OHIO, hosts more than 4,000 twins at its annual Twins Day Festival. Both identical and fraternal twins from around the world participate, and many dress alike. The twins take part in games and contests, such as the oldest identical twins and the twins with the widest combined smile. There is also a "Double Take" parade, which is nationally televised. Since twins from ages 90 to just 11 days old have attended, there are special twin programs for all age groups. The event began in 1976 in honor of Aaron and Moses Wilcox, twin brothers who inspired the city to adopt its name in 1817.

280

WORLD'S LARGEST TWINS GATHERINGS

Number of attendees

4,068	3,400	2,500	1,500	1,200
Twins Day Festival, Ohio	"Deux et plus" Gathering, France	Twins Weekend, Canada	Twins Plus Festival, Australia	Beijing Twins Festival, China

Saturday 8-5-0

State with the

LONGEST MULTIPLE-ARCH DAM

Oklahoma

With a length of 6,565 feet (2,001 m), the Pensacola Dam in OKLAHOMA is the world's longest multiple-arch dam. Built in 1941, the dam is located on the Grand River and contains the Lake of the Cherokees—one of the largest reservoirs of the country with 46,500 surface acres (18,818 ha) of water. The dam stands 145 feet (44 m) high. It was made out of 535,000 cubic yards of concrete, some 655,000 barrels of cement, another 10 million pounds (4.5 million kg) of structural steel, and 75,000 pounds (340,194 kg) of copper. The dam cost $27 million to complete.

WORLD'S LONGEST MULTIPLE-ARCH DAMS

Length, in feet (meters)

Pensacola Dam, Oklahoma	New Waddell Dam, Arizona	Daniel Johnson Dam, Canada	Florence Lake Dam, California	Mountain Dell Dam, Utah
6,565 (2,001)	4,700 (1,433)	4,297 (1,310)	3,156 (962)	800 (244)

State with the

DEEPEST LAKE

Oregon

At a depth of 1,932 feet (589 m), Crater Lake in southern OREGON partially fills the remains of an old volcano basin. The crater was formed almost 7,700 years ago when Mount Mazama erupted, and then collapsed. The lake averages about 5 miles (8 km) in diameter. Crater Lake National Park—the nation's fifth oldest park— surrounds the majestic lake and measures 249 square miles (645 sq km). The area's large snowfalls average 530 inches (1,346 cm) a year, and supply Crater Lake with its water. In addition to being the United States' deepest lake, it's also the eighth deepest lake in the world.

UNITED STATES' DEEPEST LAKES

Greatest depth, in feet (meters)

1,932 (589)	1,643 (501)	1,604 (489)	1,330 (405)	1,171 (357)
Crater Lake, Oregon	Lake Tahoe, California/ Nevada	Lake Chelan, Washington	Lake Superior, Michigan/ Minnesota/ Wisconsin	Lake Pend Oreille, Idaho

283

State with the

OLDEST DRIVE-IN THEATER

Pennsylvania

Shankweiler's Drive-In Theater opened in 1934. It was the country's second drive-in theater, and is the oldest one still operating today. Located in Orefield, PENNSYLVANIA, the single-screen theater can accommodate 320 cars. Approximately 90% of the theater's guests are children. Although they originally used sound boxes located beside the cars, today patrons can tune into a special radio station to hear the movies' music and dialogue. Shankweiler's is open from April to September.

UNITED STATES' OLDEST DRIVE-IN THEATERS

Number of years open*

74	71	69	65	62
Shankweiler's Drive-In Theater, Pennsylvania 1934	Lynn Drive-In, Ohio 1937	Saco Drive-In, Maine 1939	Sunset Drive-In Theater, Pennsylvania 1943	Hiway 50 Drive-In Theater, Tennessee 1946

*As of 2008

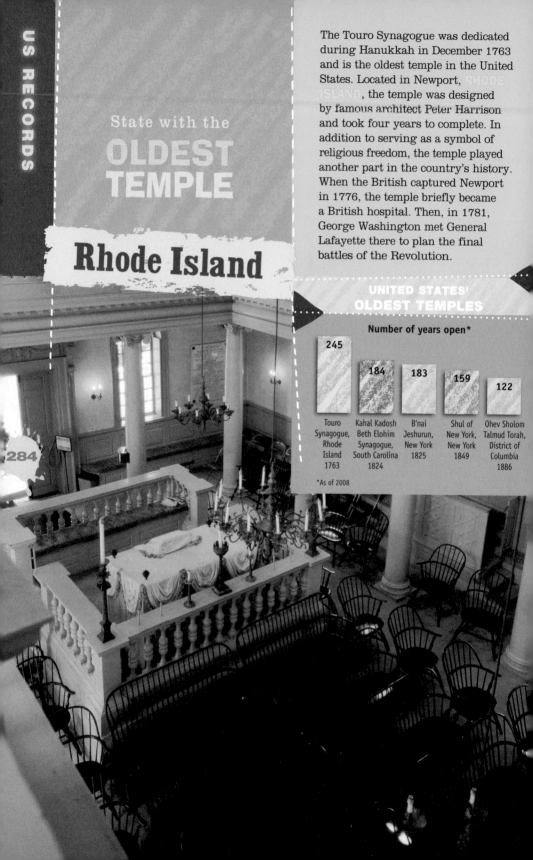

State with the
OLDEST TEMPLE

Rhode Island

The Touro Synagogue was dedicated during Hanukkah in December 1763 and is the oldest temple in the United States. Located in Newport, RHODE ISLAND, the temple was designed by famous architect Peter Harrison and took four years to complete. In addition to serving as a symbol of religious freedom, the temple played another part in the country's history. When the British captured Newport in 1776, the temple briefly became a British hospital. Then, in 1781, George Washington met General Lafayette there to plan the final battles of the Revolution.

UNITED STATES' OLDEST TEMPLES

Number of years open*

Touro Synagogue, Rhode Island 1763	Kahal Kadosh Beth Elohim Synagogue, South Carolina 1824	B'nai Jeshurun, New York 1825	Shul of New York, New York 1849	Ohev Sholom Talmud Torah, District of Columbia 1886
245	184	183	159	122

*As of 2008

284

285

State with the
OLDEST LANDSCAPED GARDENS

South Carolina

The geometrical garden patterns in Middleton Place Gardens were designed by Henry Middleton in 1741 and were modeled after the gardens at the Palace of Versailles in France. They were first opened to the public in the 1920s. Today, the gardens on this 65-acre (26.3-ha) Charleston, SOUTH CAROLINA, plantation are laid out in almost the same fashion as when they were planted more than 250 years ago. Some of the plants that are featured at Middleton Place Gardens include camellia, daffodil, magnolia, jasmine, columbine, and hydrangea. The House Museum is also located on the grounds and displays some of the Middleton family's furniture, art, and documents.

UNITED STATES' OLDEST LANDSCAPED GARDENS

Number of years since established*

267	155	117	101	76
Middleton Place Gardens, South Carolina 1741	Missouri Botanical Gardens, Missouri 1853	New York Botanical Gardens, New York 1891	Longwood Gardens, Pennsylvania 1907	Hershey Gardens, Pennsylvania 1932

*As of 2008

286

State with the
LARGEST PETRIFIED WOOD COLLECTION

South Dakota

Lemmon's Petrified Wood Park in SOUTH DAKOTA is home to 30 acres (12.1 ha) of petrified wood. It covers an entire city block in downtown Lemmon. It was built between 1930 and 1932 when locals collected petrified wood from the area and constructed displays. One structure in the park—known as The Castle—weighs more than 300 pounds (136 kg) and is made partly from petrified wood and partly of petrified dinosaur and mammoth bones. Other exhibits include a wishing well, a waterfall, the Lemmon Pioneer Museum, and hundreds of pile sculptures.

UNITED STATES' LARGEST PETRIFIED WOOD COLLECTIONS

Area, in acres (hectares)

30 (12.1)	27 (10.9)	24 (9.7)	20 (8.1)	18 (7.3)
Lemmon's Petrified Wood Park, South Dakota	Long Logs Forest, Arizona	Rainbow Forest, Arizona	Crystal Forest, Arizona	Black Forest, Arizona

Size, in square feet (square meters)

130,000 (12,077)	91,494 (8,500)	62,382 (5,795)	49,514 (4,600)	46,285 (4,300)
Tennessee Aquarium, Tennessee, USA	The Freshwater Center, Denmark	Great Lakes Aquarium, Minnesota, USA	Aquarium of the Lakes, Britain	Gifu Freshwater Aquarium, Japan

State with the LARGEST FRESHWATER AQUARIUM

Tennessee

The TENNESSEE Aquarium in Chattanooga is an impressive 130,000 square feet (12,077 sq m), making it the largest freshwater aquarium in the world. The $45-million building holds a total of 400,000 gallons (1,514,165 l) of water. In addition, the aquarium features a 60,000-square-foot (5,574-sq-m) building dedicated to the ocean and the creatures that live there. Permanent features in the aquarium include Discovery Hall and an Environmental Learning Lab. Some of the aquarium's 12,000 animals include baby alligators, paddlefish, lake sturgeon, sea dragons, and pipefish. And to feed all of these creatures, the aquarium goes through 12,000 crickets, 33,300 worms, and 1,200 pounds (545 kg) of seafood each month!

287

State with the

BIGGEST FERRIS WHEEL

Texas

The State Fair of TEXAS boasts the nation's largest Ferris wheel. Called the Texas Star, this colossal wheel measures 212 feet (64.6 m) high. That's taller than a 20-story building! The Texas Star was built in Italy and shipped to Texas for its debut at the 1986 fair. Located in the 277-acre (112-ha) Fair Park, the Texas Star is just one of the 70 rides featured a the fair. The three-week-long State Fair of Texas is the biggest state fair in the country and brings in about $350 millior in revenues annually. It is held in the fall, and the giant Ferris wheel is not the only grand-scale item there. Big Tex, a 52-foot- (15.9-m-) tall cowboy, is the fair's mascot and the biggest cowboy in the United States.

UNITED STATES' BIGGEST FERRIS WHEELS

Height of wheel, in feet (meters)

212 (64.6)	150 (45.8)	150 (45.8)	150 (45.8)	150 (45.8)
Texas Star, Texas	Giant Wheel, Ohio	Navy Pier Ferris Wheel, Illinois	Six Flags Ferris Wheel, Kentucky	Wonder Wheel, New York

288

State with the

LARGEST HUMAN-MADE HOLE

Utah

Bingham Canyon—a working mine in the Oquirrh Mountains of UTAH—is the largest human-made hole in the world. It measures 2.5 miles (4 km) wide and 0.75 miles (1.2 km) deep, covering about 1,900 acres (769 ha). It is so large that astronauts can even see it from space. Miners first began digging in the area in 1903. Today approximately 47 million tons (43 million t) of ore and 265,600 tons (240,948 t) of copper are removed from the canyon each year. Bingham Canyon is one of the largest copper mining operations in the world. It has produced more than 17 million tons (15.4 million t) of copper and 23 million ounces (652 mg) of gold in the last 100 years. Silver is also mined there.

WORLD'S LARGEST HUMAN-MADE HOLES

Width of opening, in miles (kilometers)

Bingham Canyon, Utah	Hull-Rust Mahoning Mine, Minnesota	Berkeley Pit, Minnesota	Big Hole Diamond Mine, South Africa	Rublislaw Quarry, Scotland
2.5 (4.0)	2.0 (3.2)	1.5 (2.4)	0.5 (0.8)	0.1 (0.16)

290

State that Produces the
MOST MAPLE SYRUP

Vermont

Maple syrup production in VERMONT totaled 450,000 gallons (1,703,435 L) in 2007 and accounted for about 32% of the United States' total yield that year. There are about 2,000 maple syrup producers with 2.17 million tree taps in Vermont, and the annual production generates almost $13.8 million. It takes about five tree taps to collect enough maple sap—approximately 40 gallons (151.4 L)—to produce just 1 gallon (3.79 L) of syrup. Vermont maple syrup is also made into maple sugar, maple cream, and maple candies.

STATES THAT PRODUCE THE MOST MAPLE SYRUP

Production, in gallons (liters)

Vermont	Maine	New York	Wisconsin	Ohio
450,000 (1,703,435)	225,000 (851,717)	224,000 (847,932)	75,000 (283,906)	75,000 (283,906)

THE UNITED STATES' LARGEST OFFICE BUILDINGS

Size, in millions of square feet (square meters)

6.63 (616,000)	4.40 (409,000)	2,50 (232,000)	2.10 (195,000)	1,24 (115,200)
Pentagon, Virginia	Sears Tower, Illinois	Aon Center, Illinois	Empire State Building, New York	Equitable Building, New York

State with the LARGEST OFFICE BUILDING

Virginia

The Pentagon Building in Arlington, VIRGINIA, measures 6,636,360 square feet (616,538 sq m) and covers 583 acres (236 ha). In fact, the National Capitol can fit inside the building five times! Although the Pentagon contains 17.5 miles (28.2 km) of hallways, the design of the building allows people to reach any destination in about 7 minutes. The Pentagon is almost like a small city, employing about 23,000 people. About 200,000 phone calls are made there daily, and the internal post office handles about 1.2 million pieces of mail each month.

291

State with the
LONGEST TRAIN TUNNEL

Washington

The Cascade Tunnel runs through the Cascade Mountains in central WASHINGTON and measures almost 7.8 miles (12.6 km) long. The tunnel connects the towns of Berne and Scenic. It was built by the Great Northern Railway in 1929 to replace the original tunnel that was built at an elevation frequently hit with snow slides. To help cool the trains' diesel engines and remove fumes, the tunnel is equipped with huge fans that blow air during and after a train pass.

UNITED STATES' LONGEST TRAIN TUNNELS

Length, in miles (kilometers)

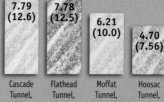

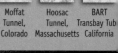

7.79 (12.6)	7.78 (12.5)	6.21 (10.0)	4.70 (7.56)	3.60 (5.79)
Cascade Tunnel, Washington	Flathead Tunnel, Missouri	Moffat Tunnel, Colorado	Hoosac Tunnel, Massachusetts	BART Transbay Tub California

292

CASCADE TUNNEL
7.8 MILES LONG   ELEVATION 2,247 FEET
41,152 FEET LONG   COMPLETED 1928

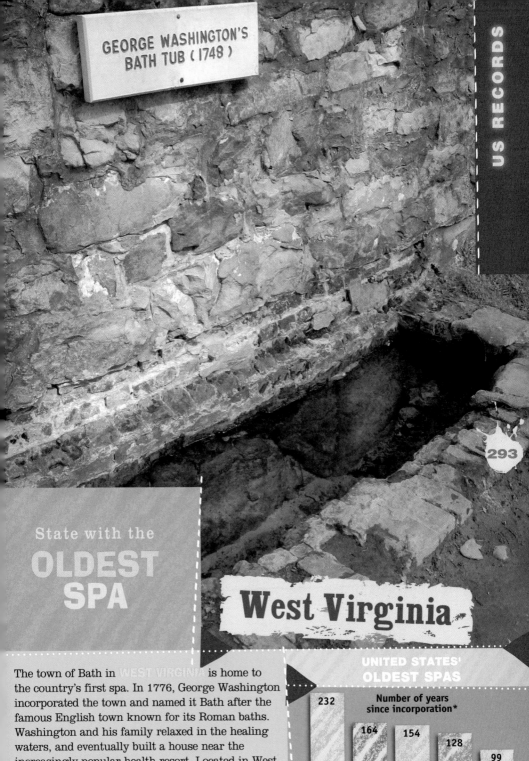

GEORGE WASHINGTON'S BATH TUB (1748)

293

State with the
OLDEST SPA

West Virginia

The town of Bath in WEST VIRGINIA is home to the country's first spa. In 1776, George Washington incorporated the town and named it Bath after the famous English town known for its Roman baths. Washington and his family relaxed in the healing waters, and eventually built a house near the increasingly popular health resort. Located in West Virginia's eastern panhandle, the Warm Spring Ridge produces about 2,000 gallons of water per minute at a temperature of 74°F. Today people come to Bath, which is also known as Berkeley Springs, for relaxation and health treatments.

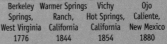
UNITED STATES' OLDEST SPAS

Number of years since incorporation*

Berkeley Springs, West Virginia 1776	Warmer Springs Ranch, California 1844	Vichy Hot Springs, California 1854	Ojo Caliente, New Mexico 1880	Steamboat Villa Hot Springs, Nevada 1909
232	164	154	128	99

*As of 2008

State with the

LARGEST WATER PARK

Wisconsin

Noah's Ark in WISCONSIN Dells sprawls for 70 acres (28.4 ha) and includes 36 waterslides. One of the most popular—Dark Voyage—takes visitors on a twisting rapids ride in the dark. The ride can pump 8,000 gallons (30,283 L) of water a minute. Visitors can also enjoy two wave pools, two mile-long "endless" rivers, and four children's play areas. It takes 5 million gallons (19 million L) of water—the equivalent of more than 14 Olympic swimming pools—to fill all the pools and operate the 3 miles (4.8 km) of waterslides. In 2006, the park's Time Warp ride opened. It's the world's largest family barrel ride, which twists riders down a 70-foot (21 m) hill at 30 miles (48 km) per hour.

UNITED STATES' LARGEST WATER PARKS

Size, in acres (hectares)

Noah's Ark, Wisconsin	Blizzard Beach, Florida	Schlitterbahn Waterpark Resort, Texas	Oceans of Fun, Missouri	Six Flags Raging Waters, California
70 (28.4)	66 (26.7)	65 (26.3)	60 (24.3)	50 (20.2)

295

State with the
LARGEST COAL MINE

Wyoming

Black Thunder Mine is located near Wright, WYOMING, and produces about 92.7 million tons (84.1 million t) of coal each year. That's about 10% of the country's total production. The mine uses a giant earth-scraping machine that can extract about 3 tons (2.7 t) of coal per second! Miners fill about 25 miles (40 km) of coal cars each day. Black Thunder—which opened in 1977—has approximately 1 billion tons (907 million t) of coal still in the mine. Black Thunder is owned by Arch Coal—one of the world's largest coal producers— and employs about 600 people.

UNITED STATES' LARGEST COAL MINES

Coal produced annually, in tons (metric tons)

Black Thunder, Wyoming	North Antelope Rochelle, Wyoming	Jacobs Ranch Mine, Wyoming	Cordero Mine, Wyoming	Antelope Coal Mine, Wyoming
92.7 (84.1)	88.5 (80.3)	40.0 (36.3)	39.7 (36.0)	33.9 (30.8)

301

303

Photo credits: Pages 6–14, 16–17, 21, 25–33, 36–38, 40, 41, 43–45, 47–51, 53–57, 59, 63–65, 68, 71, 73, 77, 82, 83, 85, 89, 90, 92, 95, 98, 100–105, 112–115, 126, 129, 131, 133, 137–140, 146–148, 150–152, 156–165, 168, 170, 172, 180, 187, 191, 202, 203, 205–207, 211, 212, 216, 233, 238–240, 244, 246–248, 251, 256–258, 261–264, 266, 268, 269, 273, 275–277, 284–286, 289, 291, 295: ©Corbis; pages 15, 18, 20, 22–24, 35, 39, 42, 58, 60, 61, 66, 67, 74–76, 135, 167, 169, 171, 173, 174, 176–179, 181, 185, 186, 189, 190, 193, 194, 197, 204, 210, 241, 272 ©AP/Wide World; pages 19, 62: ©Time, Inc.; page 34: ©Craig Blakenhorn/FOX; page 46: ©Hulton Getty/ Archive Photos; pages 70, 87, 88, 117, 123, 124: ©photos.com; pages 52, 78, 125, 186 ©Alamy Photos; pages 72, 80, 86, 96, 106, 107, 111, 118, 128, 130, 134, 136, 142–144, 154, 196, 215, 218, 200, 219–222, 250, 254, 260, 271, 282: ©Dreamstime photos; page 79: ©Cedar Point; page 84: ©Royal Gorge Bridge; pages 93, 97, 119, 122 ©Animals Animals; page 94: ©Norbert Wu; pages 99, 108, 127, 132, 145, 149, 153, 290: ©Corel Corporation; pages 109, 110, 116, 155, 223, 226–229, 259: ©PhotoDisc; page 120: ©Peter Arnold; page 121: ©Photo Researchers, Inc; pages 141, 199, 249: ©Bruce Glassman; page 183: ©Disney Corporation; pages 182, 184, 188, 209: ©Photofest; page 192: ©North Wind Picture Archive; pages 195, 198, 201, 235: ©Jen Morse; page 208: ©Vacheron Constantin; page 214: ©Yahoo!; pages 224, 225, 230–232, 234: ©NASA; page 236: ©Suzuki; page 237: ©Bob Martin/Time Inc.; page 242: ©Graeme Teague; page 243: ©Lockheed Martin; page 253: ©Robert Craig/The News Journal; page 255: ©Georgia Sports Hall of Fame; page 267: ©400 Monroe Associates; page 270: ©Uniform Photos; page 274: ©Jim Carr; page 278: ©The University of North Carolina; page 279: ©Scott Schauer; page 280: ©Twins Day Festivals; page 281: ©Elk Photography; page 283: ©Darlene Bordwell; page 287: ©Richard Bryant; page 292: ©George White; page 293: Berkley Springs; page 294: ©Noah's Ark.

Insert credits (clockwise from the top right corner of each section): Movies (page 1) Photofest; (page 2) Photofest; Television (page 1) Photofest; (page 2) Photofest, Dreamstime; Music (page 1) AP; (page 2) AP; Animals (page 1) Dreamstime; (page 2) Dreamstime; Food (page 1) AP, Dreamstime; (page 2) AP, Dreamstime; Sports (page 1) AP; (page 2) AP; Amusements (page 1) AP, Dreamstime; (page 2) AP

WILD WACKY AND AMAZING FACTS

MOVIES · TELEVISION
MUSIC · FOOD · SPORTS
ANIMALS · AMUSEMENTS

BONUS SECTION

The Write Stuff, Finally

Work first began on the script for *The Simpsons Movie* in 2003, but producers were thinking about it back in 1997 when they registered the Internet domain simpsonsmovie.com. The long-awaited script went though 158 drafts before it was finally accepted. And producers were so concerned about keeping the plot a secret, they shredded the script after every voice session.

Computer Creations

While filming *Harry Potter and the Order of the Phoenix*, producers decided it would be unrealistic to build a set for the Department of Mysteries. A physical set would have required about 15,000 crystal balls, and it would have been too time-consuming to clean and set up again if a retake was needed. So the Department of Mysteries was created digitally, and it became the first computer-generated set used throughout a movie.

Creative Crowd Control

When Prince Charming performs in *Shrek the Third*, some 1,373 different characters are in the crowd. Since the first Shrek movie, animators have drawn 4,378 different characters for the movies. To fill in the crowds, animators were able to browse the large catalog of characters. They also spent a lot of time adding details to the scenery, using 62,173 branches and 191,545 leaves per tree.

The producers of *Pirates of the Caribbean: At World's End* needed to film the shadow of the *Black Pearl* to use in the movie. To achieve this, the crew built a 65-foot (19.8-m) replica of the front of the ship and attached it to a trailer in the salt flats of Utah. The shoot was expected to take 19 days, but they finished it up in just 4 days.

Sneaky Ship Shoot

Deteriorating Dedication

For the animated picture *Ratatouille*, animators were obsessed with making realistic-looking sketches. To draw the compost pile, they brought in 15 different types of produce and let it rot. Then they photographed the stinky stuff and worked from those images. Animators also wanted to accurately capture what the Head Chef should look like when he is soaking wet. So they dressesd a man in a chef's suit and had him jump in a swimming pool. Then they took note of what parts of the outfit stuck to him and which parts you could see through.

Nutty Fans

Sometimes the fans have the last say on whether or not a TV show will be canceled. When avid viewers heard that the show *Jericho* would be ending after just 1 season, they mailed in a total of 40,000 pounds (18,143 kg) of peanuts in protest after one of the show's characters used the term "nuts" as a refusal to surrender. Producers backed down and put the show on for another season. But these types of campaigns aren't always successful. When *Veronica Mars* was in trouble, fans sent hundreds of Mars bars to producers. When they ran out of those, fans filled a tractor trailer with 14,000 pounds (6,350 kg) of Snickers bars. However, all that sweet stuff didn't sway producers to save the show.

Takes Money to Make Money

Advertisers shell out big bucks to reach viewers of TV's top shows. The most expensive is *Grey's Anatomy*, which charges $419,000 for a 30-second ad. Second place belongs to *Sunday Night Football*, which brings in $358,000 per half-minute spot. Rounding out the top 5 are *The Simpsons* ($315,000), *Heroes* ($296,000), and *Desperate Housewives* ($270,000).

Video Viewers Jump Ship

As the TV writers' strike brought new episodes to a halt from November 5, 2007, to February 12, 2008, many potential viewers turned to the Internet. More than 77.6 million people watched 3.2 billion videos on YouTube.com—about 41.6 videos per person—in 1 month. In the same month, another 40.5 million viewers saw 334 million videos on MySpace.com. Online viewers watched about 3.4 hours of online video a month, with the average video lasting 2.8 minutes.

Singing Sensation

High School Musical 2 drew 17.6 million viewers on its premiere night, not only becoming the highest-rated original movie on the Disney Channel, but the highest-rated premiere in cable history. The first movie, which stars Zac Efron as Troy and Vanessa Hudgens as Gabriella, debuted in 2006.

Musical Movie Madness

The 2008 movie *Hannah Montana & Miley Cyrus: Best of Both Worlds Concert* had the biggest Super Bowl weekend debut ever with $29 million. Even more impressive is that the 3-D movie chronicling the extremely successful tour of the same name only opened in 683 theaters and still beat out movies with a wider release. The movie averaged $42,460 per theater.

Idol Excellence

The most successful American Idols so far are Kelly Clarkson and Carrie Underwood. Clarkson, the winner from season 1, has combined album sales of 9 million copies—6 million for *Breakaway*, 2 million for *Thankful*, and 1 million for *My December*. Season 4 winner Carrie Underwood has also sold 9 million copies of her albums, including 7 million for *Some Hearts* and 2 million for *Carnival Ride*.

Top Tunes

The bestselling song on iTunes in 2007 was "Big Girls Don't Cry" by Fergie with 7.54 million downloads. The bestselling album was *It Won't Be Soon Before Long* by Maroon 5 with 252,000 downloads. For the year, a total of 844.2 million paid songs were downloaded—a 45% increase from the previous year. And 41 individual songs were downloaded more than 1 million times each—an 86% increase from 2006.

Cashing in on Christmas

Josh Groban's Christmas collection *Noel* was the bestselling album of 2007 with 3.7 million copies sold. And the album was only released in the middle of October, giving buyers just 2.5 months to purchase it. This is the first time a Christmas album has topped the sales charts since SoundScan began in 1991. SoundScan tracks sales for Nielsen by collecting data from more than 14,000 retailers.

Best of the Buckle

The CMT Music Awards have trophies that are shaped like giant belt buckles. The 2007 trophies actually had little belt buckles within them that could be removed and worn. Carrie Underwood won the most with two—Video of the Year and Female Video of the Year—for her song "Before He Cheats." After the award show aired, sales of her music jumped 24%.

One Pricey Piece of Toast

While doing a morning radio show appearance in New York in 2000, Justin Timberlake ordered French toast for breakfast. He did not finish the entire breakfast, and someone at the station saved the leftovers to put on eBay. The winning bid for the rest of Timberlake's now-mushy meal was $3,100!

Stately Snacks

Most states have an official state animal or bird, but some have taken it a step further and added official state snacks. Utah's state snack food is Jell-O. Hawaii decided that its official state muffin should be made of coconut. Texas chose the strudel as the official state pastry, and Pennsylvania opted for chocolate chip as the official state cookie. And diners looking to enjoy Massachusetts's official state pie will get Boston cream.

Diamond Dessert

When diners at Serendipity 3 in New York have some room left in their bellies for dessert, they may be tempted to order the Frozen Haute Chocolate sundae. But only if they have a lot of cash: The sundae costs $25,000! It is made from 28 cocoas from around the world and topped with edible gold. Included with the tasty treat is a diamond-encrusted gold spoon that the diner can take home.

Service with a Smile

There are 945,000 restaurants throughout the United States, and they serve about 70 billion meals and snacks each year. This results in about $558 billion in sales annually. People eat approximately 24% of their meals outside the home. The restaurant industry employees more than 13 million people, making it the second-largest employer after the U.S. government.

Big Macs for All

While visiting abroad, hungry travelers can almost always find a McDonald's to stop at. However, local menu items might catch them by surprise. For instance, New Zealanders enjoy Kiwi burgers—hamburgers topped with fried egg and pickled beets. In India, they serve the Chicken Maharaja Mac—a chicken version of the Big Mac. In Uruguay, the McHuevo—a hamburger served with mayonnaise and a poached egg—is very popular. And even on the slopes of Sweden, skiers can glide up to the McSki to enjoy hot chocolate and apple pie.

Satellite Sports

Golf is the only sport that has ever been played on the moon. On February 6, 1971, Alan Shepard hit 2 golf balls at the end of his moon walk on the Apollo 14 mission. Shepard had a collapsible golf club made for the trip, and kept it and the golf balls in his space suit. Even with the heavy gloves of his space suit, he was able to swing the club with one hand.

One Long Day

Shortstop Joel Youngblood must have been a little confused on August 4, 1982. On that day he played 2 MLB games—for 2 different teams. He started the morning as a New York Met, but ended the day as a Montreal Expo after a trade. By the end of the night, he became the first player in history to get hits for 2 different teams on the same day. He drove in the game-winning run for the Mets at Wrigley Field, and then hit a single for the Expos in Philadelphia.

Hard-Hitting

Tennis champ Andy Roddick holds the record for the fastest serve in the game. On September 24, 2004, Roddick smashed a serve at 155 miles (249.4 km) per hour to Vladimir Voltchkov at the Davis Cup semifinals. Venus Williams has the fastest women's serve, clocked at 128 miles (206.0 km) per hour. This serve came during the second round of the French Open on June 1, 2007, against Jelena Jankovic.

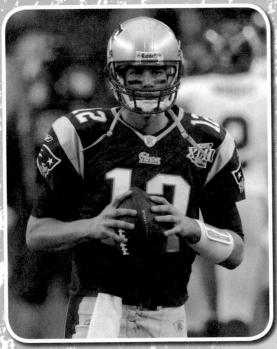

What A Birthday Present

Tom Brady is the only quarterback in NFL history to start and win 3 Super Bowls before his 28th birthday. He led the Patriots to victories in Super Bowl XXXVI when he was 24 years old, Super Bowl XXXVIII at age 26, and Super Bowl XXXIX at age 27.

Metal Mobiles

NASCAR drivers better be careful! The body of a race car is made from metal that is just 24-thousandths of an inch thick—about the same width as 8 pieces of paper. Designers can make a race car from this thin sheet of metal in just 11 days. About half of these cars are painted, and the other half are "skinned"— covered in stickers.

Jumpin' Jerboas

A jerboa is a tiny, mouse like rodent with incredibly powerful little legs. A jerboa can cover 10 feet (3.1 m) in a single jump, using its tail for balance. The tiny rodent, which is found in Africa and Asia, never drinks water. It gets all of its water from the bugs and plants that it eats.

Traveling the Tunnels

A mole can dig a tunnel that measures almost 200 ft (61 m) in just 1 night. At that pace, the nocturnal rodent could make it from 1 end of a football field and back in 4 nights. Tunneling at about 18 feet (5.5 m) per hour, a mole uses its strong front feet to push the soil out of the way. A mole makes these tunnels as it looks for earthworms and plant roots to eat.

Pounds of Poop

The average dairy cow produces 4 times its body weight in manure each year. Considering that a mature cow weighs about 1,400 pounds (6,350 kg), that's about 5,600 pounds of poop annually—or 44,800 pounds (20,320.9 kg) in a lifetime. That's the weight of about 4 monster trucks. A cow drinks about a bathtub's worth of water and eats 40 pounds (18.1 kg) of food a day.

Slimy Snacks

If you put all of the earthworms a robin eats in one year from end to end, they would stretch for 3 miles (4.8 km). In addition to worms, the birds mainly eat fruit. Robins eat worms in the morning and fruit in the afternoon. The birds are more likely to eat worms during breeding season and fill up on berries and other fruits during the winter.

Wake-Up Call

An albatross is a large shore bird that loves to fly. In fact, it rarely lands—even to sleep. The bird is able to sleep while flying at about 25 miles (40.2 km) per hour! With a wingspan of up to 7 feet (2.1 m), an albatross easily glides through the air. It only lands to build a nest, breed, and hatch an egg. From laying an egg to the time the chick is ready to leave the nest could take up to a year, so an albatross only lays 1 egg every other year.

Lots of Lunch

It takes a lot of food to keep the 1,000 animals living in Disney's Animal Kingdom in Orlando, Florida, happy. Each day, zookeepers dole out 4 tons (3.6 t) of munchies—an amount that would feed a person for 4.5 years. The animals also enjoy about 40,000 worms a week and 80,000 crickets per month. Not surprisingly, animal manure is the third most recycled product in the park!

Really Stacking Up

There are more than 15,000 Lego models made from 35 million Lego bricks located throughout Legoland in California. The largest model in the park is Bronty—a giant dinosaur made from 2 million bricks. The smallest is a duck in the San Francisco section of the Miniland area, made from just 2 bricks.

Water World

Six Flags Hurricane Harbor in New Jersey has 732,000 gallons (2,770,921.4 L) of water swirling through its Adventure River. That's enough to fill 22,000 bathtubs. Another 5,100 gallons (19,305.6 L) tip out of the giant buckets in Discovery Bay every hour. And if all the fiberglass tubing used in the park was put together, it would make a waterslide that measured 4 times higher than the Empire State Building.

Animated Animals

The carousel at Seuss Landing at Universal's Islands of Adventure is truly one of a kind. Each of the 54 creatures that guests can ride on the Caro-Seuss-El does something unique when a rider pulls the reins. Some turn their heads, some wiggle their ears, and some blink. A few of the quirky creatures include cowfish from *McElligot's Pool*, twin camels from *One Fish, Two Fish, Red Fish, Blue Fish*, and elephant-birds from *Horton Hatches the Egg*.

Going, and Going, and Going

The Steel Dragon in Nagashima, Japan, is the longest roller coaster in the world at 8,133 feet (13,088.8 m)—or about 1.5 miles (2.4 km). Located in Nagashima Spa Land, the coaster reaches a top speed of 95 miles (152.8 km) per hour and has a drop of 306 feet (492.5 m). The thrilling ride lasts for a terrifying 4 minutes.